Betrayal

of

Jesus

21st Century Challenges for Christians

Davis D. Danizier

Word Wizards, Escondido, California

Copyright © 2008-2014 by Davis D. Danizier

All rights reserved. No part of this book may be reproduced, stored in a retrieval system, or transmitted, in any form or by any means, electronic, mechanical, photocopying, recording, or otherwise, without prior permission of the author and publisher (except for brief excerpts for review purposes). Manufactured in the United States of America.

Published by:
Word Wizards®
P.O. Box 300721
Escondido, California 92030-0721
website: http://www.wordwiz72.com
ISBN Number: 978-0-944363-07-2

Cover photo Copyright © 1998-2002 "Cloudman" John A. Day
Used with grateful permission.

CONTENTS

Introduction 5

1 Betrayal 15

2 The Teaching of Jesus 19
    The Early Ministry 20
    The Completion of the Ministry 20
    The Greatest Teaching 23
    Combining the First and Second Commandments 24
    More Betrayal and Denial 25

3 The Blasphemy of Bibleolatry 27
    Contradictions 31
    Failed Prophecies 37
    Atrocities and Other Flaws 39
    All or Nothing 45
    "Triviality" of Errors Cited 46
    What the Bible IS and IS NOT 47

4 Paul vs. Jesus (and James) 49
    Faith vs. Works 52
    Paul vs. James 58
    The Law of Moses 62
    Other Problems with Paul 63
    Punishment for Adam's Sin 67
    Why Do People Follow Paul? 68

5 Bloody Human Sacrifice Atonement Mythology 69
    Focus On Greed 70
    Sinners in the Presence of God 71
    Need for a Mediator? 71
    Suffering for all the sins of humankind 73
    Paying "The Price" 74
    Sin Transference 75
    Punished for OTHERS' sins? 77
    Civil or Criminal? 77
    Jesus' Gift of Salvation 78
    The Real Process of Removing Stains 80

6	Additional Contradictions	83
7	Special Problems for Catholics	93
	Origins of Modern Christian Theology	94
	Historical Injustices	96
	Modern Injustices	99
	Issues of Doctrine, Ritual and Observance	102
	Looking Ahead	106
	Conclusions	107
8	Special Problems for Mormons	109
	Theological Integrity	110
	The First Vision and Joseph Smith's Revelations	112
	Joseph Smith and "Modern Scripture"	115
	Contradictions and Errors in LDS Scriptures	123
	Other Issues (Secret Temple Rituals, Racial Apartheid, Communal Socialism, Polygamy)	125
9	Christianity and Contemporary Issues	135
	Is Morality Declining?	135
	Is Religion Necessary for Morality?	137
	"Traditional Values"?	138
	Could an All-knowing, All-powerful, All-loving God Allow Suffering of the Innocent?	141
	Christmas and Make-believe "Culture Wars"	143
	Religion and Science; Religion in Education	147
	Religion and Politics	150
	"What if You're Wrong?"	157
	Personal Witness	159
10	Is There a God?	161
	Traditional Rationalizations for God and Counterarguments	163
	Objection to Belief in Deity and Counterargument	169
	Factors to consider	174
	Conclusions	181
	About the Author	183

INTRODUCTION

Two thousand years ago, accounts now known as the New Testament tell us that Jesus came amongst us. He was described as Jewish, a rabbi, yet also a revolutionary. He claimed that he would change not one iota or tilde from the Law of Moses[1] yet transformed that Law to unimaginable dimensions.

Jesus is reported to have taught much, yet wrote nothing. All we have of his words are the writings of those who put stylus to tablet long after his death, in an age when memories were rarely supported by written notes and could not possibly be bolstered by photographs or home videos. The earliest records of Jesus' teachings were written decades after his death and, except for Matthew, by those who had no personal acquaintance with him.

If we attempt to examine the teachings of the **real** Jesus, we must necessarily take into consideration what he actually

---

[1] Matthew 5:18

said, as preserved in the record attributed to him, and the context in which he said it. This record must be considered against the conditions under which it was created, decades after the fact.

First, we need to acknowledge that there is not any definite evidence that any **real** person such as Jesus of Nazareth ever actually existed. Such records that we have were produced decades after the fact, and even their own authorship cannot be conclusively verified and, of those, no original source texts exist, and all we have are manually copied editions entrusted to the safekeeping of powerful institutions with strong vested interests in specific dogmatic perspectives. There are no official records from the occupying Roman government (known for its detailed record-keeping) from that time period which confirm his birth, ministry or execution. There are almost no objective accounts of his existence at all from contemporary historians of the time, and none of first-hand eyewitnesses.

That said, clearly something happened in the land of Palestine in or about the year zero.

Someone taught those sayings.

Someone created such a stir that many distinct accounts exist, that were compiled separately and without collaboration, which accounts for the many contradictions and differences in the narrations presented. Clearly Mark, the first gospel writer, wrote independently of Paul's letters and apart from the much later gospel of John. Clearly, Matthew and Luke were aware of Mark and follow his account, but they were not aware of each other. Where they are similar, they follow Mark. Where they diverge (and repeatedly contradict), is in the points at which they sought to add to what Mark omitted. And then there are the apocryphal and Gnostic gospels such as Peter, Thomas, Phillip, Judas and Mary Magdalene, among others, many with original source texts preserved intact and only recently discovered (such as from the Dead Sea Scrolls from Qumran and the Nag Hammadi Library from Egypt), which also differ tremendously from those selected for the official canon, yet also tell of this remarkable person known as Jesus.

So whoever he was, whatever he was, or even if he is the fictional construct of a ghost writer, someone created a powerful message that has inspired and changed the world. "Where there is smoke, there is fire," goes the old saying. It seems difficult to imagine that so much could be written, and so much felt, without being based on some kernel of fact.

Thus, for the purpose of this book, I choose to conclude that there is something or someone we can refer to as the **real** Jesus, the source of the original teachings now attributed to Jesus, and thus will use that reference based on an attempt to synthesize the best guesses about what this **real** Jesus taught out of the records and accounts handed down to our time.

When we consider the teachings of the **real** Jesus, apart from what is widely taught by those who call themselves "Christian," we need to go back to Jesus' own words (as attributed to him in the accounts that we have). When we see the many ways in which modern religionists not only undermine Jesus' teachings but directly contradict him, we need to consider *his* original teachings, and also examine the reasons why those who profess to be his followers contradict him so directly, and how this came to be.

This book is necessary because a serious response is needed to both of the ways in which many who call themselves "Christians" actually undermine the real Jesus — from one side by those who dismiss him altogether and from the other side by those whose deeply sincere but seriously misguided devotion leads them away from what he actually taught and, instead, toward a superficial worshipfulness that seeks to glorify him in words while actually dishonoring him by contravening his teachings and rejecting the real gift that he actually left for them (and all of us).

We need to understand not only the ways in which many who call themselves Christians do undermine and directly oppose the teachings of the real Jesus, but also why this happens and how the original message of Jesus got corrupted into something so unrecognizably contrary. Certainly those who call themselves Christians are sincere and well-intended and have no desire to be out of sync with the one they consider to be the messianic begotten son of god.

Many who have looked at these words in print or on our web site have jumped to inaccurate conclusions about the tone and intent of these writings, as well as to incorrect conclusions about my purposes and background. Because I raise serious questions about forms of worship or specific traditional beliefs that are widely considered to be essential for those who claim to accept Jesus' gift, some have wrongly interpreted these writings as an attack on Christianity. I want to make it very clear that this is *not* an "anti-Christian" work, and is not meant to attack or insult the deeply-held beliefs of Christians.

It is, however, clearly my intent to challenge the beliefs of so-called Christians whose form of worship and belief is misdirected and give them something to think about that they probably haven't seriously considered before. Clearly I hope that my sincere affection for this person of Jesus and his wonderful teachings shows through, especially as I defend his original message against the attacks both from within the ranks of his self-professed followers and those who reject him altogether (largely because their perceptions of him are inaccurately derived from how he is portrayed by those who claim to follow him), beginning with the "apostle" Paul, to whom the earliest and strongest attack on Jesus' teachings can be traced and who I believe has done more to undermine Christianity than anyone else in history.

Contrary to the conclusions of many who have read my earlier writings, I do not hate more traditional Christians, though I vigorously challenge the teachings of conservative Christian sects such as the "evangelical" or "born-again" Protestants, Catholics and Mormons. I was raised as a conservative Christian and grew up believing the Bible to be the inerrant and infallible word of God. I was active in Christian youth groups and during my teenage years converted other friends to my faith. Most of my family and many of my closest friends maintain a strong and abiding faith in more traditional Christian beliefs and believe me to be sadly in error, but because they know me personally and know that I am sincere, they tolerate me with the hopeful optimism I will return like the lost sheep to the fold (hmmm, perhaps the "sheep" metaphor is appropriate here).

I am not a trained minister and have not completed formal theological or seminary studies. I do not consider myself to be a Bible expert.

But in my lay studies of the Bible, and limited formal teaching (including some seminary), I encountered many specific problematic discoveries such as direct internal contradictions, prophecies that covered specific events that passed without the prophecies being fulfilled, and statements that are simply wrong based on modern knowledge that was not known to the primitive ancients.

Betrayal of Jesus

As I encountered such issues, my initial assumptions were that simple answers must exist and that I was obviously missing something. But when I innocently raised my questions and concerns to responsible and educated persons I looked up to, they responded first with simplistic answers that didn't address the points I had raised and, when I pursued with follow-up questions, they reacted as though I were some kind of radical heretic seeking to undermine all the teachings of Christianity. I gradually and reluctantly came to accept the truth that, while there is much good in the Bible and in Christian teachings, especially those attributed to Jesus himself in Matthew and Luke (the refined synoptic gospels), that the Bible could not be seen to be inerrant or infallible and Jesus could not be seen as a messiah or Christ. This discovery was traumatic for me, but I felt it necessary to gird up the necessary moral courage and bravely confront error instead of sweeping it under the carpet or running away from it in cowardice as many are tempted to do.

It soon became clear that the main reason for my traditional Christian faith was not that it was "true" in any grand cosmic sense, but because it was the one that had been taught to me at my mother's knee and thus felt right to me in a deep and meaningful way. The fact became clear that when serious questions of factual error and internal contradiction arose, those I turned to in my own faith could not offer answers better than those in any other faith. If I would not accept such flawed responses from others, then I should not accept it from my own.

But what about the many miracles of Christianity? The personal relationship with Jesus Christ as Savior? The burning in the bosom as the Spirit whispers confirmation of Biblical truths? I had experienced the depths of religious experience and it was too real to deny. But I also observed that such

INTRODUCTION

religious experience was not limited to my own faith. Others in every faith have experienced the same whispering of their God attesting to their truth. The power of this religious experience is very real, but cannot be seen as objective reality because it is common to all faiths, "confirming" competing beliefs, and motivating such passion that adherents will die (or kill) for their beliefs. The experience of religious conviction may be real, but it is the motivating factor behind the most violent wars and the worst bloodshed and hatred in all of history.

To confront such truth — that my cherished Bible and faith were not the perfect messages from God that I had believed in — was a traumatic experience. All areas of my life, my family, friends, social life, were centered in my religion. I was not one of those "wild youths" who sought escape from piety in orgies of sex, drugs or rock and roll; on the contrary, I was a quiet, thoughtful youth, active in church activities and Bible study, and very comfortable in the religious experience which had meant so much to me.

But I had to be honest.

The purpose of this commentary is not to "debunk" the Bible or Christianity or to try to take away from satisfied Christians something of value that they cherish.

First, it should be noted that I hold the Bible in high esteem. It is an important and authentic relic of legitimate antiquity that deserves honor, and is the basis on which the moral traditions of the Western World were founded. It provides tremendous insight into how people lived in ancient times, and what they thought, and how it led to the development of modern traditions. It is also brings the message of well-written moral masterpieces — the best efforts of ancient, primitive writers who also offer amazing insights into human nature and ethics. True, there is much cruelty and harshness, especially in the Old Testament. But there is also much love, beauty and morality that still resonate with truth today. Just as we can learn moral lessons from the ancient writings of China, India and even the Greek fables and myths, there is much of truth in the Bible if we seek it out selectively, using the same appropriate judgment that we would in analyzing the value of our contemporary writers.

Second is my strong admiration for Jesus and the teachings that are attributed to him in the gospels, especially the synoptic gospels of Matthew, Mark and Luke (John was written much later, is more strongly influenced by Paul, and is of the most questionable authenticity). However imperfect or incomplete the account may be, what comes through from the various accounts is the clear vision of an important man, with important ideas about morality, peace and goodness, presented in a way that rings true today and strongly backed up by insights from modern disciplines such as psychology, philosophy and other social sciences. Clearly Jesus (or whoever devised the teachings attributed to him) left us a tremendous free gift, if only we have the wisdom to recognize it, distinguish it from other writings of those who came before him or after him, and accept it.

Unfortunately, this love and beauty that fill the words attributed to Jesus were severely undermined by Paul, who taught a message 180° opposite of Jesus. And since Paul was the missionary through whose perspective so many converts found their way to Christianity, the tragedy is that it is his view that becomes the dominant view of Christendom. As a Roman citizen, Paul had the unique ability to travel freely throughout the empire and become the "great missionary" and thus it is through him that "Christianity" expanded and

Introduction

therefore through the filter of his prism that the light of Jesus' teachings is distorted.

Third, I see a resurgence of those who seek to unravel the carefully crafted separation of church and state that was the genius of our Founders, and which enhanced the integrity of both church and state. Today I see many conservative Christians trying to create an official religion in our secular nation. They do not have confidence that others will be attracted to their brand of harsh, cruel Christian teaching rooted in Paul rather than Jesus on its own merits, but that it requires authoritarian government coercion to force itself onto others. Ironically, the same conservatives who express little confidence in the government to handle other matters are quite content to let government dictate matters of faith; they seem to place more trust in the government to decide matters of conscience than in their churches, families and private religious schools. It is incumbent on all free people to resist the intursion of public institutions into the most private of personal domains. The last time the Church dominated the Western world, we called it the Dark Ages. Today, many of those with the same mentality seek to resist and obstruct science and reason and return us to that era of dark reliance on superstition. It is hoped that this effort can help expose some of the reasons why such primivitve thinking must be rejected.

Fourth, I do not seek to take anything away from contented, respectful Christians who do not seek to impose their private beliefs on others. This is evident in the manner in which I handle the information I have to offer. I do not aggressively market my message to Christians; I do not hunt them down in their places of worship or seek them out to engage them in dialogues or debates. I do not create online advertisements, or send out bulk junk mail, whether as online

Betrayal of Jesus

"spam" or via the Postal Service. If those in the Christian faith are happy and content, so be it. However, many are not happy with modern Christianity. They chafe under its rules and restrictions, and they are uncomfortable with the way it seeks to proselytize its message to others, by vigorous preaching (even to the unwilling) or even by seeking control of political agendas to force their values on the unwilling. In their hearts they suspect something that doesn't add up, but they can't quite put their finger on it. They seek answers to their questions. I do not go out looking for disaffected Christians, however I have placed notice of its availability in the places they are likely to find it — but only if they go looking for it. I make the information available to those who want it, whether they be the uncomfortable Christians or those who go looking to debate. I don't seek out debate partners, but if they come looking for me I am well prepared to discuss my positions.

I sincerely hope that my tone of respect and of genuine admiration for many of the teachings attributed to Jesus and the Bible's historical importance will come through in what I have written. I also know that many will think me hostile to their faith and take everything I write as a personal insult.

But I need to remind them that I do not "interpret" the Bible; I cite its own words and let its truth, beauty and, yes, its contradictions and flaws stand on their own.

We need not judge the Bible. We need only let it speak for itself as we evaluate the modern conclusions and doctrines others seek to derive from it.

DAVIS D. DANIZIER
San Diego, California

1

Betrayal

The story of Jesus' betrayal by Judas for thirty pieces of silver is a familiar one. Judas becomes the ultimate Bible villain who sells his role as trusted confidant to the Savior in exchange for a pittance of earthly wealth and, in shame, hangs himself in an ignoble death.

Yet some have argued that Judas did not betray the Savior. If Jesus' purpose for existence was to come to Earth as the Son of God and die for our sins, then it was necessary that this death occur, and Judas' act made this possible. If Judas had not set Jesus up to be captured by Roman soldiers, tried by the priests of establish religious orthodoxy, and then crucified by his enemies, then the Christian sacrifice might never have occurred and those who believe this act by Jesus atoned for human sins would be left without their mediator.

No, the act of Judas made Jesus' sacrifice possible.

The act of Judas was not the great betrayal of Jesus.

But betrayal there would be.

Betrayal of Jesus

The true betrayal would be on a scale far more grand than what most Christians could ever imagine. The "betrayal" by Judas (which made possible the sacrifice on the cross that many Christians deem necessary as the central mission of a messianic Jesus) pales in comparison to the real betrayal, accomplished on a grand scale and embraced by the very Christians so quick to condemn Judas.

The real betrayal was perpetrated by those who came after Jesus and, in his name, transformed his simple, loving, joyful message into one of violence, greed, domination and conquest — a caricature of all he stood for that contradicts his message and which he would have found unrecognizable. And the betrayers have taken as their profits far more in wealth, land and power than a mere 30 pieces of silver.

This book seeks two important objectives:

1. Identify the real teachings attributed to Jesus, and show how they apply in a modern context to our lives today, at both personal and social levels.

2. Identify the ways in which those who profess to be the teachers of Jesus' message fall into the trap of those who betray Jesus. Many modern teachers of so-called "Christian" teaching are devout and sincere, well-meaning and humble servants dedicated to that which they sincerely believe to be true. Their sincerity, however, does not make them right.

I understand that many will find my writings to challenge their traditional beliefs. Such readers must understand that I came from the same background that they do. Nevertheless, they may find my comments threatening and perhaps even heretical. No problem. I once felt the same way and I understand their reluctance to challenge their views based on the words of a stranger. I certainly would never have changed my views just because a stranger asked me to.

So I don't ask you to reconsider your opinions based on the word of a stranger. Look to an authority you trust.

Do you believe the Bible to be the inerrant/infallible Word of God? Well, we will need to examine this assumption further, but for now let us just say that if you accept the Bible as the inerrant/infallible Word of God then you will accept the words of Jesus as recorded in the four gospels (Matthew, Mark, Luke and John) as the authorized record and most reliable account of what Jesus said and what teachings should be attributed to him.

I know it will be difficult for many to see things in a new light, from a different perspective. So don't trust me. Go to your Bibles. I assume that every traditional Christian who reads this has a Bible in their home, probably more than one, and probably more than one version or translation. So don't trust me. **Trust your own Bibles!** Every time I quote a verse that seems incredible to you, *don't trust me!* **Trust your own Bibles! DON'T TRUST ME!** Don't trust me — or your minister. Go to your own Bible. Pull it off the shelf. Dust it off if you have to. Open it up and look inside. Every time I make a claim about what the Bible says, I cite the exact chapter and verse. Thus it is easy for you to look up for yourself and see what is already right there, in your own Bible. Don't trust me, or your priest, or your favorite Bible author. Read it for yourself. Look in your own Bible and then see who is telling you the truth.

Again, I was raised as a conservative "born again" evangelical Christian. I modified my views of what it truly means to be a follower of Jesus because of what I read in the Bible. Not what someone else told me, but what is in the Bible. Again, don't take my word for it. I'm sure you have your own Bible. Don't trust anyone else. Pull your own Bible off the shelf, and see that I'm not making this up!

Betrayal of Jesus

If you accept the premise that the four gospels represent the most reliable accounts of what Jesus actually taught while on this earth, then join with me in examining what Jesus actually taught, and then let us compare that with the teachings and doctrines of fundamentalist evangelical Christian sects (or cults) who call themselves after the name of Jesus but whose teachings are far from what He gave us. They draw near to Jesus with their lip service (as he warned), but their hearts are far from what He really taught (Matthew 15:8 and Mark 7:6).

So join with me as we examine the record of teachings attributed to Jesus, and then compare them to the modern teachings of those who claim to be His followers.

2
The Teaching of Jesus

Jesus was a revolutionary. He was a Jew, a rabbi and, while he claimed in Matthew 5:18 that he would not make the slightest change in the Law of Moses, he taught a new perspective on the ancient Law that would transform it forever for those who understood the real depth and meaning of his message.

The teachings attributed to him were both simple and radical, and apart from what they may or may not offer in terms of salvation in a world hereafter, they do teach a manner of living that brings peace, happiness and salvation in this life that can only add to the quality of whatever additional dimensions lie ahead in our futures.

The life-transforming message that he brought is offered as a free gift. It is ours for the taking, if only we will recognize it and accept it. It is an offering of pure love and grace. And he gave it in a time when the manner of his teaching put

Betrayal of Jesus

him at great odds with the established religious orthodoxy — the conservative religious establishment — of his day. He taught at great risk and he was fully aware of that risk to his personal safety, which ultimately cost him his life. He knowingly risked his life to give us this free gift.

He gave his life for this gift, so the least we can do is recognize it and accept it as he meant it, not through the distorted interpretations of those who came later.

For this we must turn to those accounts of Jesus' own teachings, not those of his later followers.

The Early Ministry

To fully grasp the fullness of Jesus' real gift and message, we must look at it in the total context of his ministry, from the first teachings to the last teachings and to his own statements about the priorities of values.

Near the beginning of his ministry, in the Sermon on the Mount, Jesus first pays homage to the Law of Moses (Matt. 5:18) but then goes on to expand on it in new and revolutionary ways. He preaches meekness, mercy and peace (Matt 5:5-9). He taught love not only of neighbor but also of enemies, and to "turn the other cheek" (Matt. 5:39-44). In many other ways he took the letter of the Old Testament Law of Moses and emphasized the spirit of the law. He also chastised the religious orthodoxy by asserting that true religion should be a purely private matter, not a public issue (Matt. 6:1-8) and gave us the Golden Rule (Matt. 7:12).

The Completion of the Ministry

At the close of Jesus' earthly ministry, in his last recorded teaching prior to going to the upper room for the Last Supper and beginning the sequence of events that would culminate in

The Teaching of Jesus

his betrayal arrest, trial and crucifixion, Jesus wrapped up his message with the *only* time that he, himself, describes the final judgment. Note that many who call themselves Christians read Matthew chapter 24 in which Jesus describes the signs of the "last days" or "end times" and spend endless hours in fascinated discourse on what this means, but often fail to turn the page to Matthew 25 to read Jesus' own account of the final judgment.

Near the end of chapter 25 (verses 31-46), Matthew reports Jesus' teaching that the Son of Man shall come and divide the "sheep" from the "goats." The righteous He will welcome to eternal life, "...for I was hungry and you gave me food, I was thirsty and you gave me drink, I was a stranger and you welcomed me, I was naked and you clothed me, I was sick and you visited me, I was in prison and you came to me." At this, the righteous ones are astounded and puzzled. They look upon the great God Almighty, in all his splendor on the Throne of Eternity and can't remember when they ever saw this all-powerful deity hungry or thirsty or a stranger or naked or sick or in prison, and in any case can't imagine what they, in their puny condition of mortality, could possibly have done for him anyway.

The almighty tells the righteous, "...as you did it to one of *the least one of my brothers,* you did it to me." His final general teaching, the closing words of his earthly ministry, define the standard of salvation. This passage identifies *universal compassion, expressed actively through deeds,* as the criterion for eternal judgment. And within a few hours he would be betrayed, arrested, tried and *crucified.*

The ancient practice of crucifixion is one of the most cruel means of execution ever devised. It involves stringing the human body up in a position where the person's full weight is supported only by the outstretched arms, and then leaving

Betrayal of Jesus

him to hang like that until the intense pain finally kills him through a slow process of internal suffocation. Even an expert gymnast in top physical condition has only enough strength to withstand the position of a suspended cross for a few moments. But when the body is fastened in place with ropes or nails (according to differing local customs), so that it *can't* drop, it lingers in intense pain for two or three hours until it succumbs to an agonizing death.

That was the kind of cruelty that Jesus was forced to endure in his final moments of mortality. To be sure, his execution was a painful event.

He was a sensitive man who watched as one of his most trusted companions betrayed him with a kiss and another denied even knowing him. He was hurriedly tried by despotic officials of the contemporary religious orthodoxy, who made a travesty of justice. He was forced to carry his own heavy cross through a jeering mob so hostile that even his closest associate denied even knowing him. While other criminals with him were tied to their crosses with ropes, he was nailed to his cross with spikes driven through his hands and feet. He asked, in his agony, for water, and they gave him a sponge filled with vinegar. He hung on the cross for more than three hours in the painful process of death by crucifixion.

Under such conditions, we could certainly understand if the pressures of that agony caused him to erupt in anguish or fury. Yet he was able to reach selflessly to those nearby, and direct himself through compassion for them to overcome the self-directed compulsion of his agonizing pain, and pass on in peace.

Moments before his death, at the height of physical agony, he spoke with compassion for his tormentors: "Father, forgive them; for they know not what they do." (Luke 23:34)

The Teaching of Jesus

The Greatest Teaching

Somewhere during the middle of his ministry, a lawyer challenged Jesus to identify the "great commandment in the law." As a Jewish rabbi, Jesus answered from existing Old Testament law, "You shall love the Lord your God with all your heart, and with all your soul, and with all your mind. This is the first commandment. And a second is like it, You shall love your neighbor as yourself. On these two commandments depend all the law and the prophets." (Matt. 22:36-40 and Luke 10:25-37; compare also Deuteronomy 6:5 and Leviticus 19:18 for the Old Testament origins.) In the Luke version, Jesus then gives the parable of the Good Samaritan, defining "neighbor" in the broadest possible terms, as the Samaritans were hated enemy; *the **non-believer;*** the most despised minority group. Perhaps if Jesus were to return to Israel today, he would substitute "Palestinian" (and for many of the same reasons the Jews of Jesus' era hated the Samaritans). The parable of "The Good Palestinian." If Jesus were speaking to whites in South Africa [or America of the 1950's], he might refer to those with different skin color. If speaking to Catholics in Northern Ireland, he might substitute Protestants, or Catholics if speaking to Protestants.) Jesus clearly states that these two commandments — love of God and our neighbor (broadly defined to include enemies) — are the foundation on which everything else is based.

The time may come when many self-professed Christians might stand before Jesus, but will not be awarded the gift of salvation. They will protest, "But I accepted You as my Savior!" And Jesus will answer, "You spoke words of acceptance, but you did not accept me. Many times I came to you and you turned me away. You saw me as a homeless beggar and turned away in revulsion. I was sick with AIDS and you refused to come near me. I was a stranger, from a different

Betrayal of Jesus

country, without proper papers, and you welcomed me not. I came to you as the 'least of these,' *and you accepted me not."* Jesus closed out his first teaching, the Sermon on the Mount, with a warning that it is not enough to profess acceptance with lip service only (Matt. 7:21-27). True acceptance is *demonstrated in action,* not just empty words.

The salvation of unconditional love, called "agape" love in ancient Greek, began His ministry, ended His ministry, and the basis for everything else.

Combining the First and Second Commandments:

Many of those who claim to be followers of Jesus demonstrate their obedience to the first commandment, to love God, with endless choruses of Hallelujah or constant chants of "Praise the Lord," as if God were some egomaniac who depends on the empty words of praise from mindless sycophants. Such "Christians" need to go back and read the New Testament again, and see how the pieces fit together in an overarching context. Jesus had a consistent theme.

There is nothing we puny mortals can do for the Almighty king and creator of the universe. *He does not need our praise!* To the Creator of the Universe, the best efforts of puny human mortals would be worthless! There is nothing we can possibly do for him! The best efforts of our own righteousness would be as "filthy rags" (Isaiah 64:6). But Jesus made it very clear exactly what he *does* want. The first commandment is fulfilled in the second: showing our love of God through kindness to the "least of these."

When we show love to our fellow beings, we are expressing that love to God, not *our* way, but the way *He* requested in Matthew 25:31-46. *"As you did it to one of the least of these my brethren, you did it to me."* (Note, this is the last gneral teaching Jesus gave in his ministry before going up for the Last Supper and the end of things; it is the *only* time Jesus himself ever describes the final judgment. This is an important passage.) Mother Teresa has interpreted this sentence very literally. It is the slogan for her Missionaries of Charity, and the first among her "Declaration of Basic Principles." She grew up in comfortable conditions in Europe, as an Albanian. As she developed an understanding of the way in which this sentence summarizes the ministry and message of Jesus and links the first and second great commandments, she sought to identify the very least of these, not just in her own city or country or even in Europe, but in all the world. She found them in the streets of Calcutta, India. Giving up all she had, she went to live among them, serving them in compassionate joy, ultimately establishing centers in the most poverty-stricken centers of urban squalor in the world. She says, "It is Christ in His distressing disguise whom I love and serve."[1] In the face of each starving infant she pulls from the urban trash heaps of Calcutta, or each impoverished, dying elderly stranger she comforts, she sees the face of Jesus. Through our loving service to others we "do it unto" God.

Nothing we can *do* offers tangible benefit worthy of the Creator. The intangible radiance of heart-felt compassion is the gift he requested, and the praise offering he seeks.

More Betrayal and Denial

When seen through the perspective of the long view, with a comprehensive picture of Jesus' overall ministry and teachings, from the first to the last and to what he personally

---

[1] Mother Teresa, *My Life for the Poor,* (San Francisco: Harper & Row, 1985) p. 95.

identified as the first and greatest of the teachings, it could not be more clear what Jesus taught and what he gave to us.

Yet this is not the teaching of some modern Christian sects. Many of those who call themselves followers of Jesus hold beliefs that are completely opposite of what Jesus taught. Where Jesus taught universal love and compassion expressed in actions, many modern "Christians" hold narrow-minded, often hateful attitudes toward minorities and foreigners; where Jesus taught salvation through compassionate deeds, many modern "Christians" teach that salvation is not based at all on what one does, but only on one's beliefs.

In calling themselves after the name of Jesus while teaching and practicing the opposite of Jesus' actual message, these so-called "Christians" perpetuate the betrayal by Judas and the denial by Peter. In their lip service affirmations of belief, acceptance and empty professions of "faith," they reject Jesus' real gift. They are those of whom Jesus foretold in Matt. 15:8 and Mark 7:6, when he warned of those who draw with their lips but their hearts are far from him.

So how did this complete rejection of Jesus by those who claim to be his followers become so widespread and prevalent throughout established Christianity?

The answer lies with the manner in which Christianity spread from being a tiny, provincial, local movement to a worldwide phenomenon. And for that it needed a leader who was educated, wealthy and had the papers and means to travel widely.

The greatest betrayal of all, more than that of Judas or Peter, would come from the "apostle" Paul.

3

The Blasphemy of Bibleolatry

The Bible is an amazing compendium of ancient wisdom and lore that has been handed down to the present world from its Bronze-Age origins at the hands of primitive sheep herders and fishermen. For some, it is seen as being divinely inspired and inerrantly infallible, while others dismiss it for its harsh cruelty, misogynistic paternalism, atrocities of the worst nature attributed to commands from God, and point to its many internal contradictions and factual errors in rushing to dismiss it as a fraud. As a result, the true nature and history of this remarkable artifact are often lost into the arguments about the extremes of calling it either a cruel hoax or a divine miracle.

All too often the Bible is seen in terms of all-or-nothing, black-and-white extremes, often summarized by the question: *"Is the Bible true?"*

Betrayal of Jesus

But as Pilate asked Jesus (John 18:38), "What is truth?" And, what is the truth about the Bible?

There are many who are quick to dismiss it as a fraudulent package of worthless myths, while others proclaim it to be the inerrant, infallible Word of God. But can it neatly fit into either simplistic stereotype?

Is the Bible a fraud?

If someone were to come forth today and claim that they had discovered a new work dating back to Bible times, whether that era is defined in terms of the period written about or the more recent period to which we can trace the origins of actual preserved texts, the first question would *not* be as to whether every statement in it were factually accurate. It would be to determine, using whatever scientific and analytical tools possible, whether the document actually came from the time and place claimed and if it were really written in the ancient times and places of the Bible. We would try to determine its authorship and compare its contents with those of other documents whose authenticity as ancient documents has already been confirmed.

This is the same thing we would do if newly-discovered texts were claimed for the legends of the Greeks, Romans, Vikings, Mayans, Incas or any other ancient compendium of mythology.

In that context, as to the legitimacy of its claims to be of legitimate ancient authenticity, there can be little doubt in terms of modern Bible scholarship, evaluation of documents preserved, and the historical record of those documents' origins, that the Bible is clearly the work of ancient writers. As such, it clearly gives us a window into the thoughts of ancient peoples from whom much of modern ethical thinking has developed.

The Blasphemy of Bibleolatry

At the same time, the same can be said of the mythologies of the ancient Egyptians, Greeks, Romans and the civilizations of ancient India, Africa, Mesoamerica and Asia. Archeologists and anthropologists treasure the insights that verified discoveries of ancient documents provide about those ancient civilizations and how they thought and lived. Yet, though treasured and revered, few would seriously consider those writings to be the inerrant, infallible Word of God merely because they are really, really old.

Thus the Bible, and whatever insights and wisdom can be found in it, must incontrovertibly be accepted as a great gift to the modern world. But that, alone, does not make it the infallible, inerrant Word of God — a claim that would have to be evaluated separately on its merits.

It should reasonable be expected that any work that would claim authorship or inspiration from a deity described as omniscient (all-knowing) and omnipotent (all-powerful), would — reflecting the character of its primal source — be completely devoid of any flaws or imperfections. In fact, one of the claims that has often been made on behalf of the Bible by some of its more simple-minded proponents, is that it consists of 66 books produced over a span of some 5,000 years by more than 40 different writers and yet does not have a single contradiction or flaw in it. As we shall see, this claim is, sadly, far off the mark.

For all the richness, insight and wisdom which the Bible provides, we must remember that it came forth from a people who began their existence as nomadic refugees, first from the lands of the fertile crescent, later from Egyptian slavery, and also from subsequent conquests by Babylon (Persia) and Rome. The books of the Bible were produced at differing times, under differing conditions, by writers who often did not know of each other and were not familiar with each other's works. The Bible itself was not even compiled into its current form until several *centuries* after the last event in it (other than prophecies) had occurred. The early Christians did not go to their worship services carrying their neatly-packaged Bibles — the Bible was yet be developed and, in those early times, differing communities of Christians (not to mention the Jews from whom the Old Testament of the Bible originated) had very different and sometimes conflicting compilations which only a few could actually possess in those days before inexpensive printing and production methods. Not until early in the fourth century A.D. did councils of mortal men *vote* to decide which books would be *in* and which would be *out* in the final compilation of a standardized Bible. (And even today the process is not fully agreed upon, as Catholic and Protestant Bibles have differing numbers of books, and varying translations of the Bible include or exclude various contested passages.) It is ironic that many Evangelical Bible literalists claim that Catholics are not true Christians, yet they claim divine infallibility of a specific set of ancient writings selected and compiled by the very body whose theology they find fatally suspect.

The result, predictably, is a book which, when carefully examined, presents us with many stunning and direct contradictions, not to mention obvious errors of fact and logic which we would expect to be unknown to ancient primitives but not unknown to an omniscient deity revealing its contents. Additionally, just as any fortune-teller has many success stories to brag about (as well as a good number of failed predictions to try to sweep under the carpet), so the Bible, in its human frailty, also has many stunning successes in its prophecies (though some might have actually been written long after the events predicted actually occurred), but even the edited version that has come down to us also

The Blasphemy of Bibleolatry

contains many glaring examples of prophecies in which events were predicted in a specific time frame or context, and that context has passed while the prophecy has NOT been fulfilled as predicted.

Let us examine each of these areas (contradictions, failed prophecies and flaws):

Contradictions

1. The very first page of the Old Testament opens right up with contradictory descriptions of the creation (Genesis 1 vs. Genesis 2). For example, if the Institute for Creation Research sought relevant information from Genesis, would they determine that plants were created, then animals, then humans (Genesis 1), or humans, then plants then animals (Genesis 2)? Note that in both passages, time indicators are clearly established.

In Genesis 1 God's creative handiwork for each day is described in order. In verses 11-13 it clearly states that plants were created on the third day. In verses 20-25 it clearly states that fish and birds were created on the fifth day and land animals on the sixth. In verses 26-31 it clearly states that humans were created on the sixth day, after the land animals had been formed. First plants, then animals then humans.

In Genesis 2 there is a different and contradictory sequence (many Bible scholars believe these were two separate traditions that were consolidated into a single book). In verses 5-7 it says that *before any plants had been created (for there was not a man to till the ground)*, that God first formed the heavens and the earth and then created man. It specifically states that this came first and even states the reason. In verses 8-9 it says that God then planted a garden "eastward in Eden," and put the man there to care for it, and planted every kind of tree and plant. But it was not good for man to be alone in the garden, so God decided to provide companions and, in verses 19-20 God created companions. So the creation sequence is: first man, then plants, then animals. (And as a side note, this primitive God of the early writings, who would become more decisive as the traditions evolved, decided that these animals didn't quite provide enough companionship, so he decided to provide a female companion which seems to have proven much more satisfactory. Shouldn't an "omniscient" [all-knowing] deity have already known this?)

At its most simple, the contradiction between Genesis 1 and Genesis 2 can be stated as: Genesis 1 says that the humans (male and female) were created last, after animals. Genesis 2 says that the man (male) was created first and animals were created much later for the purpose of being the man's companions, but that didn't work out so well (God's error) so, lastly, God created a female human who turned out to be much more companionable. Well, at least until she listed to that darn talking snake and turned out to be somewhat rather naughty (sinful).

So aside from completely lacking in any of the scientific evidence that accompanies, say, evolution (supported by DNA evidence and extensive transitional fossils), aside from the fact that there is absolutely no evidence whatsoever to support the myth of a talking snake in a magic garden, the accounts right in the first two chapters can't keep their story straight.

2. Likewise, the very first page of the New Testament introduces another major contradiction: inconsistent genealogies of Jesus' ancestry in Matthew and Luke.

The Blasphemy of Bibleolatry

Some have "explained" this discrepancy by claiming that Luke is the genealogy of Mary; such a claim acknowledges error, since Luke specifically states that it is the genealogy of *Joseph* [Luke 3:23], just like Matthew [Matt 1:16]. So, either there is a contradiction (Matthew says that Jacob is the father of Joseph; Luke says Heli is the father of Joseph, and from there back to Solomon not a single name is the same; not even the same number of generations), or Luke makes an incorrect statement of relevant fact.

Many readers have written to defend the claim that Luke is the genealogy of Mary, but that the Bible says that Heli is the father of Joseph because women were not regarded equally with men in the Bible record, and that the father of Mary is also the father of Joseph, which we in modern times would call "father-*in-law*." But if we look at the actual historical context of such usages in the Bible, this explanation is quickly shown to utterly fail.

Wherever the Bible identifies prominent women and cites their relationship to their husband's families, it uses the term "in-law." Anyone who owns a digital Bible (on a diskette or CD or on your hard drive) should do a quick search on the expression "in-law" and see how routinely this is used throughout both Old and New Testaments to identify that relationship (e.g., Sarai, wife of Abraham, Ruth, and many others). Women are identified both as to their fathers-in-law and, for men, to their daughters-in-law, throughout the Bible. And when the lineage of a woman is identified it is her own ancestors that are cited, as in the case of Esther (see Esther 2:5-7; notwithstanding that Esther then married the King who would certainly provide her with a fine lineage of his own, if things were counted that way). Is Mary, *the mother of Jesus,* less important than others such as Sarai, Esther or Ruth? If *their* in-law relationships or genealogies can be included, why not Mary's? And, can you find one single other example in the Bible where a lineage is cited through the woman but it says someone was the "father of" and then gives her husband's name instead of her own?

Please also note that translations prepared by professionals take into consideration the context of cultural variations. Perhaps one might claim that the scholars of the King James (almost 400 years ago) were not sophisticated to reflect these cultural implications; however more recent updates (Revised Standard Version, New International Version, Today's English) have excellent standards of professionalism in developing scholarly translations, and every one of them identifies Joseph as the SON of Heli, and not one of them has concluded that Heli was the father-in-law of Mary.

3. In fact, the entire accounts of the birth of Jesus in Matthew and Luke are not only completely inconsistent, but also include direct contradictions.

Here are examples of details in Matthew but not in Luke:
- Wise men from East bring gifts (Matt 2:11)
- King Herod is on the throne at the time of Jesus' birth (Herod's reign ends in 4 BC) (Matt 2:1) and kills all babies under age two (Matt 2:16) though there is no other external historical source, Jewish or otherwise, to confirm what would have been a horrendous holocaust.
- After the birth, Joseph and Mary flee immediately with Jesus to Egypt (Matt 2:13-15)
- Note: there is no manger, no shepherds, no Roman census, no travel to Bethlehem (they seem to just be there already) and no story of John the Baptist's birth, and no mention of the reign of Quirinius (Cyrenius) in Syria, which did not overlap at any time with the reign of Herod.

The Blasphemy of Bibleolatry

Here are examples of details in Luke but not Matthew:
- Story of Zacariah, Elizabeth and John the Baptist's birth (Luke Chapter 1)
- Decree of Caesar Augusts for a worldwide census (Luke 2:1), which is not supported by any corroborating historical account.
- Mary and Joseph travel from Nazareth to Bethlehem (Luke 2:4).
- Birth in a manger because there is no room in the inn (Luke 2:7; 2:12).
- Shepherds (Luke 2:8-20) and angels (Luke 2:13-15)
- After the birth, they linger in Jerusalem for circumcision, blessings, etc., and then return directly to Nazareth. (Luke 2:21-39).
- Birth occurs when Cyrenius [KJV] (aka: Quirinius in NIV, RSV and historical accounts), whose reign began in 6 AD.
- Note: there are no wise men, no mention of Herod and no flight to Egypt.

The ONLY overlapping details are the angelic annunciation and that it happened in Bethlehem, which was needed to satisfy Micah 5:2, which is often interpreted by Christians as being a prophecy of Jesus.

More significant are the direct contradictions:
- Matthew notes that Herod, whose reign ended in 4 BC, is on the throne of Judea (Matt 2:1), while Luke claims that Quirinius (or Cyerenius) is ruler of Syria (Luke 2:2), but that reign did not begin until 6 AD, ten years AFTER Herod had left the throne of Judea as claimed by Matthew!
- Further, Matthew claims that after the birth, Joseph and Mary immediately take Jesus and flee directly to Egypt (Matt 2:13-15), while Luke claims they linger in nearby Jerusalem for Jewish rituals and then return directly to Nazareth (Luke 2:21-39).

It is certainly probable that two different reporters covering the same events would pick and choose different details or which minor aspects to emphasize. That is not the case here. It is not a matter of telling similar stories with only a few differing details or points of emphasis. They are telling completely different stories.

4. Apostles James and Paul disagreed about a key doctrine: whether "salvation" is by faith alone, or faith and works combined. Compare the direct contradictions (when analyzed for parallel vocabulary and parallel grammatical structure in the original language) in wording between Romans 3:28 and James 2:24.

Additional scriptures support faith alone (Romans 3:27-28 & 4:6; II Timothy 1:9; Ephesians 2:8-9; Galatians 2:16; Titus 3:5), while others specify the need for works / good deeds (Matt 16:27, Revelations 2:26 & 20:12; 2 Timothy 4:14; Philippians 2:12; James 2:24-26).

The ultimate contradiction of the Bible is the deep division between the two key figures of Christianity: Jesus, revered as savior and god/man; and Paul, the apostle who spread the infant religion of Christianity throughout the known world. The depth of their contradictory disagreement is so intense, and so fundamental to the most basic Christian doctrines, that it merits a separate and deeper analysis, which is provided in Chapter Four.

These are just a few examples of contradictions that leap quickly to mind. A longer compilation entitled "Biblical Contradictions," with *hundreds* of such contradictions (and still incomplete!), can be downloaded as a text file by visiting our web page at: **http://www.wordwiz72.com/contr.txt** and in Chapter Six of this book.

Failed Prophecies

1. Ezekiel [chapters 26-28] erroneously predicts that during the reign of King Nebuchadnezzar [Ezekiel 26:7] the city of Tyre will be *utterly destroyed*, become a *bare rock* [Ezekiel 26:4; 26:14 — KJV says "like the top of a rock"; NIV says "scrape away the rubble and make a bare rock"], and *never be rebuilt* [Ez 26:14; 26:21]. The city was defeated in battle in 587 BC, during King Nebuchadnezzar's reign, but was **not** "utterly" destroyed or "never rebuilt." In fact, Tyre today has more than 20,000 inhabitants at the core of the "old city" (on the original site), surrounded by a metropolitan area of more than 100,000 people! (Even within Bible times, long after the battle described by Ezekiel, Tyre had already been rebuilt and, in New Testament times it is still portrayed as a *city* (Mark 3:8) and as a harbor where ships could unload (Acts 21:3,7), so this could also qualify as a *contradiction*.

2. Matt 12:40 clearly says: "For as Jonas was three days and three nights in the whale's belly; so shall the Son of man be three days and three nights in the heart of the earth." Please note it says *three days **and** three nights* (the same as in Jonah 1:17 which it refers to). Yet *all four gospels* report that Jesus died on Friday evening and was resurrected on Sunday morning (at or before dawn, some more contradictions on this point), which would only allow less than 36 hours, not three days AND three nights.

Other than the reference in Matthew 12:40 seeking to link Jesus to an Old Testament reference, the gospels use the phrase, "On the third day" instead of "three days and three nights" (Matt 16:21; 17:23; 20:19; Mark 9:31; 10:34; Luke 9:22; 18:33; 24:7), to reflect the chronology of death of Friday (first day), in the tomb Saturday (second day), resurrection Sunday (third day) as recounted in all four gospel accounts.

Betrayal of Jesus

3. In Matt 24:34 Jesus predicts that the end of the world and all the fantastic "signs" he describes will occur within the lifetimes of the "current generation" or those currently living at the time Jesus spoke those words.

Paul and Jesus didn't agree on much (see Chapter 4 for many specific contradictions between Jesus and the renegade "apostle" Paul), but they both share this failed prophecy. In addition to the verse from Jesus cited above, this failed prophecy is reinforced even more explicitly by Paul in his epistle to the Thessalonians, in I Thessalonians 4:15-17 which makes it clear that Jesus is prophesied to return within the lifetimes of those still alive at the time the epistle is written.

Even ignoring Paul's much more specific statements in Thessalonians, some have written to claim that the reference in Matthew is to the generation in which the signs and wonders begin, not the generation contemporaneous with Jesus. However, there is absolutely nothing to suggest that the reference to generations also refers to a "future" generation. Jesus is referring to a time indicator of when in the future those future events will occur. He says it is in the future, but before *this generation* passes away. Those who claim the future reference say that means when the sign starts, *"that generation"* will not pass. But the scripture says *"this"* generation (proximal), not *"that"* generation (remote). Jesus does not talk about a "future" generation. He uses the term "this" which refers to an immediate or current reference. In fact some other versions of the Bible, notably "Today's English Version" (developed by Reader's Digest) actually say "the generation now living" which is how their professional translators chose to convert the clear and unambiguous source references into modern English. Translators of most other versions seemed content to leave it with the immediate pronominal referent "this" generation which, in the absence of a more remote referent or specific future reference, makes it clear and unambiguous that the reference is to the people of the contemporaneous generation which Jesus is addressing).

4. Isaiah 7:14 is widely claimed as a prophesy for a messiah, who shall be given the name "Immanuel." This must not be referring to the son of Mary and Joseph, since they did *not* name him Immanuel, but rather, Jesus. The only reference to the name Immanuel in the entire New Testament is Matt 1:25 referring to Isaiah's prophecy, but even Matthew never actually uses that as a name or reference to Jesus and, in fact, there is no Bible record of Jesus being named or even ever called or referred to as "Immanuel."

Similarly, Isaiah 53:5-12 is often cited as a prophecy of Jesus' atonement and his taking upon himself our sins. In reality, it has nothing to do with anyone taking upon himself anyone else's sins, nor is it even remotely related to Jesus. Verse 5 states that the victim described is "wounded" and "bruised with stripes" (terminology that describes a flogging but not a crucifixion). It says nothing about the victim dying — on the contrary, verse 10 explicitly states that this unfortunate victim will live a long life (Jesus died young) and see his offspring (Jesus reportedly died childless, unless you accept the "DaVinci Code" hypothesis). Since Peter makes the connection between this passage and Jesus (IPeter 2:24-25), this can also count as a contradiction.

Atrocities and Other Flaws

Numbers Chapter 31 *commands* the Israelites to invade the Midianites (verse 1-2), the chapter goes on to describe the cruelty, destruction and taking of spoils of war *commanded by god*. It says God *commands* the killing of every adult male, and this was done (verse 7). When they return with the male children and females, they are *commanded by god* to kill all the male children and all the females who "have known man intimately," which is Bible language for not being virgins (verse 17).

Further, it tells this bunch of horny warriors, as part of their spoils of war, to keep alive the virgin girls "for yourselves" (verse 18) For what? To baby sit them? Why just the girls and not the boys? Why only virgins? Why is their sexual history relevant? Putting it into historical context, and given what we know of the culture of that time, and the tradition of rape and pillage allowed by conquering warriors for military spoils, in that context it clearly appears that, according to the Bible in this passage, God (through Moses) is **commanding rape!** (Verses 30-35 showing the command was carried out). Some have claimed that the Midianite virgins that the soldiers were instructed to "keep for themselves" means the soldiers were to marry them. However, the Bible has no record of wholesale marriage between the Israelite soldiers and Midianites. And verses 32-35 of this chapter refer to the captured virgins as "booty" (in the King James Version; the New International Version uses the term "plunder"). It does not refer to them as "brides." In any case, why would they need only brides; after all the men lost in battle, seems they would be more in need of young men if marriage was the object. And after the soldiers have just killed their fathers, mothers, brothers and any sisters who weren't virgins, I'm sure they can really look forward to loving marital bliss (at least the Israelites won't have to worry about "in-law" problems, but one would think a compassionate God would have more consideration for these poor girls).

Deut 22:28-29 "[28] If a man happens to meet a virgin who is not pledged to be married and rapes her and they are

The Blasphemy of Bibleolatry

discovered, [29] he shall pay the girl's father fifty shekels of silver. He must marry the girl, for he has violated her. He can never divorce her as long as he lives. (NIV)." In no way is the rape victim given a choice. The marriage *must happen.* Perhaps she had refused his proposal! All he has to do is *rape* her and she's *trapped* for the rest of her poor, miserable life, *with the person who violated her,* no matter how righteous and virtuous she had tried to live. She is a double victim.

Exodus 22:18 *commands* the killing of witches. Lev 20:27 (KJV) commands the killing of *wizards* (including Oz?)

Exodus 35:2 clearly states that those who work on the Sabbath should be put to death. Which of the Bible believers is personally willing to execute those with Sunday jobs?

Additional requirements for the death penalty include gays (Leviticus 20:13), adulterers (Lev. 20:10), or nonbelievers (2 Chronicles 15:12-13). I would ask my friends who believe the Bible to be literally commanded by God:

- Are you personally willing to stone, hang or burn those who claim to be (or you just suspect of being) witches?
- Are you personally willing to stone, hang or burn someone who violates the Sabbath?
- Are you personally willing to stone, hang or burn anyone you know who has ever committed adultery?
- Are you personally willing to stone, hang or burn someone for being gay?

Leviticus chapter 21, verses 17-24, makes it very clear that those with a variety of disabilities are not welcome to approach the altar of God. Will Bible believers initiate a campaign to overturn the wicked Americans with Disabilities Act? Verse 20 specifically mentions any defect or "blemish" in one's vision. I wear prescription glasses. How far from perfect 20/20 vision are we allowed to deviate?

BETRAYAL OF JESUS

Deuteronomy 23:1-2 *commands* that men who become genitally mutilated be rejected as outcasts, and that a bastard (the innocent child of illicit sexual relations) be outcast "even to his tenth generation." (No wonder abortion was practiced, and permitted in the law — Numbers 5:12-28 — and in fact, is not prohibited or even discouraged anywhere in the Bible, as discussed in greater depth in Chapter 9: *"Christianity and Contemporary Issues."*)

2 Kings 2:23-24 shows that God, through his prophet Elisha, causes two she-bears to attack 42 "small boys" simply because they made fun of Elisha's baldness. Additionally, Deuteronomy 21:18-21 commands that parents discipline a disobedient son by stoning him to death. Strict observance of these scriptural commands could do much to streamline the backlog in our juvenile justice system.

Judges 11:29-40 God's covenant with Jephthah requires him to give his virgin daughter as burnt offering, and it is done. Not only is this offering of a virgin as a human sacrifice (of his own daughter!) extremely barbaric, it also directly contradicts the prohibition in Deuteronomy 18:10 against allowing one's own "son or daughter to pass through fire."

Beyond contemporary issues such as creationism vs. evolution, the Bible contains many other simple errors of fact regarding science and nature: Leviticus 11:6 asserts that hares chew the cud like cows; they do not. Deut 14:18 classifies bats as birds; they are not birds, they are mammals. Leviticus 11:20-23 describes flying insects such as beetles, grasshoppers and locusts as having four legs; they have six. Not surprisingly, those promoting the Bible as the sole authority on science avoid some of these more embarrassing verses.

The Bible is pro-slavery. There are many examples in the Old Testament where slavery was approved by God; it was even *commanded* that captives in war be taken as slaves (Num 31; Joshua 9:23). Leviticus 25:44-46 outlines the do's and dont's of permissible slavery. Verse 46 specifically permits slavery, as long as fellow Hebrews are not the slaves. In Genesis 9:25-27 God commands Canaan to become a slave (the word "servant" is used in King James Version; the word "slave" is used in the more modern Revised Standard and New International Versions). In the kinder, gentler New Testament, Paul wrote that slaves should be obedient to their masters (Eph 6:5-7 & Titus 2:9-10). In I Peter 2:18, it is even specified to be submissive both to masters who are overbearing as well as gentle! Why didn't they speak out against this moral outrage? Were they afraid of the law? They could at least have remained neutral on the subject.

Leviticus gives some excellent examples of flaws and contradictions. For those who claim that the Mosaic Law was superseded/replaced by Jesus' higher law, or that Christians are under mercy and not law, I would just say: don't go around using the usual passages from Leviticus (18:22; 20:13) to condemn homosexuals if you don't endorse all of its commandments with equal enthusiasm.

Leviticus chapter 11 enumerates permissible and forbidden foods. Permitted are cloven-hoofed cud-chewing animals such as cows and lambs (v.3); forbidden are cloven-hoofed non-cud-chewing animals (camels, etc.); additional animals prohibited as meat include rabbits (v.6), *pork* (v.7). Verses 8-9 specify that fish with fins and scales are permitted, but all other seafood (specifies both seas and rivers) is an *abomination*. So I hope none of you Bible-lovers who are too fond of shrimp, crab, lobsters, oysters, and other shellfish., are feeling too cramped by the *Law*. And it is not just a matter of "law" — foods such as shellfish and pork are described as an *abomination*. So even if you believe the *Law* to be superseded, that would no make these "unclean" dietary products any less "abominable" than anything else so described in Leviticus. Actually, I recommend the entire 11th chapter of Leviticus to anyone who takes the Bible too literally.

Lev chapter 12 describes a woman's uncleanliness during and after menstruation, and ritual purification for women. I hope all those women who cite Old Testament commandments against anything are strict in the obedience to these rituals. Of course, since they can't speak in Church (1Cor 14:34-35), we don't need to hear them griping about it.

So again, those who cite the Law of Moses to condemn homosexuality, show themselves to be selectively cherry-picking scripture, ignoring the prohibitions against the things they choose to indulge in. Similarly, falsely citing the Bible as the basis for "traditional marriage" of one man and one woman ignores the fact that through most of the Bible, the definition of marriage was one man and multiple prepubescent underage women, who were considered his chattel property (see additional information and references in Chapter 8). And if you want to follow strictly the Biblical definition of "traditional marriage," it also means that a rape victim must be forced to marry her rapist (Deut 22:28-29). Fortunately, marriage has been *evolving* and being redefined for millennia.

Here is a real-life example so absurd it seems like a joke, but really happened. I recently received in my office P.O. Box a brochure just addressed to "Business Manager" at my address. It was from an organization called "The Geocentric Bible Foundation, Inc." The headline title blares: "Have Scientists Been Wrong? For 400 Years?" By starting with the premise that the Bible is the literally factual, inerrant and infallible Word of God, it cities Biblical verses to claim that

The Blasphemy of Bibleolatry

the sun revolves around the earth and not the earth around the sun. While most of even those who believe in Bible inerrancy or even Bible literalism would allow for some allegoric or metaphoric references and would not accept either the Biblical citations or the interpolated conclusions from them, it does show how far afield one can go if one starts from the flawed premise of Biblical inerrancy and infallibility.

All or Nothing

A number of readers have written to say that the Bible must be accepted as true in its entirety or else it is entirely false.

I do not understand this "all or nothing" extremist mentality. Why do they hold the Bible to this extreme standard, but not other works? I read many books. In each, I accept some parts and reject other parts. There are many great philosophers or writers whose ideas I mostly admire, but I can't think of a single one with whom I am in 100% agreement with on absolutely detail they teach. Just because I may disagree with them on occasional details does not mean I reject other points that are valid. If I think them wrong on a few points, it doesn't mean that I must therefore completely cut myself off from all their other good points.

If Christians find a few flaws in the minor details of works by contemporary Christian writers, I'm sure they can overlook these little errors as the works of fallible mortal humans and still accept the main points that agree with their beliefs. Likewise, I believe that Jesus and some of his followers taught many worthy lessons. But they were human. They were doing the best they could an sometimes did a pretty good job. That there are flaws just proves their humanness, but does not mean that because they are imperfect they are therefore evil or entirely wrong on all details.

Betrayal of Jesus

The existence of a few minor flaws, some contradictions, and other failings does not discredit the importance of what these ancient thinkers developed with the limited resources available to them in their primitive societies. It only becomes problematic for those who claim that the writings of these ancient philosophers are not merely the works of wise old men but the inerrant, infallible word of an omniscient, omnipotent deity. Having made that claim, it is problematic for them to explain how a perfect, infallible deity could have left divine scripture which, in fact, can be clearly shown to have the flaws and errors that we would expect from a work written by mortal humans. The result is that they become forced to resort to convoluted reconciliations and tortured mental gymnastics to try to explain why the Bible doesn't actually mean what it clearly does say.

"Triviality" of Errors Cited

Some have written to claim that the Bible errors I have cited are minor or trivial. I have cited many errors, here (see Chapter 6) and on my website with a link to *hundreds* more. Some are on significant points of doctrine or important points of theology. Many, perhaps most, are indeed trivial. But that isn't the point. If one believes that the Bible is God-breathed, authored or inspired to be inerrant and infallible, then to be inerrant or infallible means *no errors*. It must be as perfect as the omnipotent deity claimed to have inspired it.

The claim that errors are "trivial" is a tacit admission that the Bible that we have does contain imperfections. It doesn't really matter if the details are minor or the result of clerical errors. The Bible we have is not the perfect, inerrant, infallible word of god.

The Blasphemy of Bibleolatry

Based on both the original context and the plain, simple words that have been handed down to us in whatever translation, that there is no possible way of explaining away the contradictions, factual errors and failed prophecies.

But even if, in some cases, there might be a possible (not plausible, but merely "possible") way in which a contradiction might be construed to mean something different than what it seems to mean, even with all their contortions of fact, logic and language, the idea that this process of mental gymnastics has to be exercised hundreds of times to make sense of the Bible that has been handed down to us means that, to everyday people, it becomes functionally worthless insofar as it claims to be the perfect and inerrant word of god as opposed to the collective wisdom of the ancients who laid the foundations for modern ethics, law and culture.

What the Bible IS and IS NOT

But the real question is: What does the Bible itself say about its own "infallibility"? Actually, it says nothing. The Bible in its current compilation didn't even exist until several centuries after the last book was written. Why are religious zealots so quick to claim divine authorship of a book that doesn't even claim it for itself (with the exception of specific portions of law and prophecy such as "Thus sayeth the Lord...," but not to the modern Bible as a whole)? The Bible was a collection of separate writings (laws, plays, poems, songs, histories and letters) by individual religious commentators who never imagined their writings would ever be considered divine. They are just like modern writers, making commentary and analysis, who just happened to have their works assembled and voted on by later believers who then canonized their words. They refer to the sanctity of sacred scripture (the body already canonized before their time — such as the

Betrayal of Jesus

Law of Moses and the writings of the Old Testament prophets) never imagining that someday THEIR writings, letters, or whatever will be added to the canon. Paul the Apostle, who clearly believed that the established scripture of his day was inspired (see 2 Timothy 3:16), also clearly acknowledged that some of his own writings were NOT, as when he wrote in 1 Cor 7:12 "But to the rest speak I, *not the lord...*" (emphasis added); and 2 Cor 11:17 "That which I speak, I speak [it] *not after the lord...*" (emphasis added).

It is not necessary for good Christians to accept the Bible as the inerrant or infallible Word of God in order to understand and believe in Jesus' teachings of universal compassion. After all, the early Christians themselves did not have an "infallible Bible" to carry around with them — it wasn't even compiled until centuries later. Just as we gain insights and understanding from modern writers and commentators of today, without claiming that they are divine and infallible, we can gain insight and understanding from ancient writers, as long as we consider their works for what they are, with critical thinking and common sense — not just blind faith.

We should accept the Bible for what it is: often wise and inspirational, but many times filled with error and cruelty. It is an important historical relic, and the original source for much of Western ethical theory, but its words must be analyzed and evaluated on their merits — as the writing of men, not of God. It does not claim to be anything more.

So ... on to a deeper analysis of the premier contradiction: the disagreement between Paul and Jesus on some of the most fundamental issues of Christian theology.

4

Paul vs. Jesus (and James)

In the early decades following Jesus' death, his followers remained a small, local sect. They retained their Jewish identify and, in fact, only Jews could be baptized as new followers, as "Christians."

Although this nascent Christian movement was clearly a faction of Judaism, many Jews felt threatened by their challenges to the established orthodoxy and the many radical new doctrines that were taught. And this resulted in much persecution of Christians by some (but by no means all, nor even a majority) of the Jews.

One of the early persecutors was named Saul of Tarsus. He had the rare status of being both a Jew (the people conquered by the Romans) as well as being a Roman citizen. It is lost to history how he obtained such status; it is speculated that perhaps his father had saved the life of a Roman leader and was thus rewarded, or in some other way gained favor. In any case, as an orthodox Jew he was loyal to the traditional teachings, and as a Roman citizen of means he had the freedom (and documents) and the means to travel anywhere throughout the Roman Empire.

Subsequently, Saul claimed to have had a dramatic vision on the road to Damascus and claims to have miraculously converted to this new cult he had been persecuting, in which it was Saul who held the coats of those who stoned the martyred apostle Stephen (Acts 7:58; 22:20). To signify his new life, he renamed himself from "Saul" to "Paul." Because of his education and status, Paul was very impressive to most of the founding Christians who were mostly uneducated fishermen and shepherds, such as Peter and John, who are described in Acts 4:13 as being "unlearned and ignorant" (King James), which was written by gospel-writer Luke, a presumably-educated physician. (A couple of notable exceptions are James, the brother of Jesus, and Matthew, the Publican. In addition to being educated, these are two of the New Testament writers who had lived closest to Jesus during his actual lifetime and ministry.)

Through the centuries, Paul has enjoyed widespread, uncritical adulation by those whose views are shaped by listening to others instead of thinking for themselves. In contrast, many independent-minded analyses of how Paul deals with Jesus' teachings are much more ready to find fault with Paul. One of the most famous critcisms comes from Thomas Jefferson, who wrote in a letter to William Short dated April 13, 1820, and repeated in a letter to James Smith dated December 8, 1822, that "Paul was ... the first corruptor of the doctrines of Jesus." George Bernard Shaw, the English playwright, is widely quoted as having said: "...it would have been a better world if Paul had never been born."

Paul vs. Jesus

Despite his education and eloquence, which come through so clearly in his extensive writings (more prolific than any other Bible writer and fully one third of the New Testament), Paul manages to completely contradict and undermine the teachings he claims to have become converted to and becomes more a renegade than an "apostle."

Why is it that Paul's many letters (epistles) so consistently and repeatedly contradict and undermine the teachings attributed to Jesus? Perhaps this admitted persecutor of Christians found a more effective way to subvert the followers of Jesus. Perhaps he infiltrated their ranks and taught a doctrine that opposed Jesus, replacing Jesus' selfless teaching of universal compassionate action with a selfish teaching of desire to gain a "free gift" of salvation based only on faith and completely devoid of any behavioral requirement or obedience to law, thus distracting us from the selfless teachings of Jesus.

It is impossible to look into the mind of a man long dead and determine his motives conclusively. Was he a sincere and loyal convert who simply misunderstood the teachings of his new master? Or did he have a more sinister intent to subvert and undermine the teachings of him who he claimed to be the messianic savior? We'll never know. What we can say with certainty, however, is that after examining the legacy of writing he left — more than any other writer in the Bible — that, for whatever reason, intentional or a great historical misunderstanding, the message he left opposed and undermined that of the titular messiah (Jesus the "Christ") to whom he claimed obeisance. The evidence becomes apparent when we compare the words of Paul side by side with those attributed to Jesus (who left no writings of his own) and to the other followers closest to Jesus, such as his brother James.

Let's examine the record:

Faith vs. Works

On the critical religious matter of just what it takes to attain salvation, what Jesus teaches is very different than what is written in the words of the renegade "apostle" Paul.

While Paul teaches a salvation based solely on faith *and not one's deeds,* Jesus reportedly teaches the opposite: that *behavioral* requirements (works/deeds), rooted in an internal change of spiritual growth within the person, though the gift of teaching and techniques to achieve this personal change are a gift of grace not earned or deserved by us, but requiring *actions* [deeds] to implement), are integral to salvation.

Some will say that puny mortals can never perform enough good behavior to "earn" salvation based on the value of their deeds — that the attempts at human righteousness is as "filthy rags" (Isaiah 64:6). While perhaps it is not possible for us to "earn" the "free gift" that Jesus *did* give by teaching universal compassionate love that transforms our evil selfishness into a more holy kindness of love, Jesus clearly includes a behavioral component to his requirements for "salvation." While he does not say that this satisfies any "debt," he still requires it; perhaps he is demanding merely a small partial "payment" as a gesture of "good faith." (In fact, James suggests this by his comments in James 2:26, that we demonstrate our faith — if it is genuine — *by* our deeds.)

Aside from the fact that this simply contradicts Jesus, the point is not whether or not our puny mortal attempts at righteousness have intrinsic value or not. Just as a child may offer its parents an awkwardly-drawn piece of art, which likely holds little real artistic merit (in terms of art critics it might be as "filthy rags"), still the parents sincerely and genuinely cherish such efforts. It may not "merit" winning any serious art award and may be able to "earn" very little, but loving parents accept it for its true and lasting value.

Paul vs. Jesus

Why would a loving god, as a more perfect spiritual father, not be able to give even greater acceptance, even of "filthy rags," if sincerely offered as the best effort ... *especially* if he has said that he would do so? To argue against that is to join Paul in contradicting the teachings of Jesus.

In his *first* public teaching (the Sermon on the Mount) Jesus introduces a bold new concept, not only that we should love friends and neighbors, but our enemies as well.

When asked by a lawyer what the most important commandment in the *law* was, Jesus answered (as reported in Matt 22:36-40 and Luke 10:25-37) with references from the Old Testament, that the *greatest* law was to love god (see Deut 6:5) and the second was to love your neighbor as yourself (see Lev 19:18). In the Luke text, the lawyer specifically asks what is necessary for eternal life (verse 25) and after Jesus references the two *great* commandments, he says "This *do* and you will live" (verse 28) — showing clearly that salvation is related to works/deeds/ actions, however important faith might be to motivating such behavior. Note further, that in the Luke version, this was illustrated by an example, the parable of the Good Samaritan, which was used to define "neighbor" very broadly, to include enemies. The Samaritan is the one who exemplifies this broad definition, and who provides the example of one who is saved by their compassionate actions toward their enemy. Yet **the Samaritan is not even a believer,** not one having "faith" and **not one who has accepted Jesus as savior,** yet this is who Jesus chooses as the example of one who gains eternal life, which is what the lawyer specifically asked.

Another time during his ministry, Jesus taught that the people who would go to heaven (be saved) must be as little children (Matt 18:4-5; 19:14; Mark 9:36-37; 10:14-15; Luke 18:15-17), while Paul wrote that maturity demands us to forsake the things of childhood (I Cor 13:11). Thus, while Jesus teaches us that the kingdom of heaven will be filled with those who lived their lives in active compassion and childlike innocence, Paul envisions a heaven of crusty, serious "mature" grouches who merely have to profess "acceptance" of Jesus without ever actually performing a single kind, compassionate, cheerful or childishly playful deed.

In his *last* public teaching, Matt. 25:31-45, Jesus describes the final judgment as being based solely on behavioral responses to internalized compassion. And Jesus makes it very clear that those who *do* express universal compassion in behavioral action *will be saved,* and those who do not will *not* be saved. Period. There is no other qualification.

As noted earlier, Mother Teresa juxtaposed these two messages (the "great commandments" and that what we **do** to "the least of these" is done to God) to postulate that our actions toward "the least of these" are actually done unto god, which she took very literally, and asserted that we fulfill the first commandment by obedience to the second — which motivated her to give up a well-to-do life in Albania, and search to find whoever was the ultimate "least of these" in the world, which she found first on the streets of Calcutta, India, and later in missions throughout the world.

Dr. Viktor Frankl, a German Jew who survived the Nazi concentration camps during the Holocaust, wrote in his book *Man's Search for Meaning* of rare but remarkable examples of men in the concentration camps who, dying of hunger, still gave comfort, along with their last crusts of bread, to their fellow sufferers to alleviate their suffering. Even torture and extreme deprivation could not cause them to abandon their deeply-felt compassion. But those prisoners described by Frankl were Jewish. They haven't confessed Jesus as their savior. Paul would consign them to hell (eternal torture — "fireboarding"? — worse than the universally condemned cruelty of waterboarding at Guantánamo Bay or Abu Ghraib) for even the slightest infraction) while Jesus would embrace them and count them among His sheep. The same thing also applies to the many Buddhists, Hindus and Pagans who express deep compassion in their lives who Jesus' teaching welcomes into Eternal Glory, but who Paul consigns to eternal flames of Hell. Paul subverts Jesus' joyful teaching of love and compassion and replaces it with a vision of eternal harshness and cruelty.

And, speaking of hell, we need to consider the very concept of "hell" — of eternal flames burning the flesh painfully but never consuming it, just burning painfully forever, never ever allowing the victim to be put out of his misery. Civilized societies around the world condemn torture even for the most heinous acts. To believe that a loving, compassionate god would consign people to the eternal torture of hell just because, without having been exposed to any direct evidence, and perhaps absent even the opportunity to have heard of him, they did not believe in him during this mortal lifetime. Try to imagine the sweetest, kindest, most loving and most Christ-like person you know. Do you think they rise to the level of God's own compassion? Do you think, just maybe, God is even *more* compassionate and loving? Can you envision this sweet, loving person being the one to pour fuel over the body of another conscious human person, and then lighting the match and personally igniting the painful flames of torture? And then letting it run on? Forever? Do you really believe a "loving" deity could do this?

And for what heinous crime? Murder? Torture? Rape? Kidnapping? All of the above? No. It is merely because someone simply didn't "believe." Didn't join the team. Even if they lived in deepest Africa hundreds of years before Jesus was born and never even had a chance to hear about him. This is a demand for pure primitive tribal affinity; nothing more, nothing less.

Please understand why I cannot believe in the silly nonsense of such a primitive, barbaric little deity fashioned by the primitive, tribalistic barbaric savages who invented him in their image.

Another issue must be considered when contemplating a theology of salvation based solely on belief in Jesus as the Savior and nothing else. Belief requires exposure; one cannot believe in something that one has never been exposed to. So what about those who were supposedly created by a God who is both just and merciful, but lived in a time or place when there would be absolutely no possible chance of ever being exposed to Jesus? Imagine an innocent child born in India, China or Africa 800 years before Jesus was born (or even 800 years afterward, for that matter). There would be absolutely no chance this child could ever be exposed to the opportunity of believing in Jesus or accepting him as personal savior. Again, Paul's theology consigns such innocent children to hell, while (as noted previously) Jesus taught that of such is the kingdom of heaven (Matt 18:4-5; 19:14; Mark 9:36-37; 10:14-15; Luke 18:15-17), while (as noted previously) Jesus taught that of such is the kingdom of heaven (Matt 18:4-5; 19:14; Mark 9:36-37; 10:14-15; Luke 18:15-17). Is Paul's doctrine of salvation only by faith, and consigning all others to eternal damnation, from the God of justice or mercy?

Even in John 3, the discourse to Nicodemus on salvation as a gift of grace, Jesus includes specific behavioral requirements (John 3:19-21). In any case, while some writings (other than Paul) may occasionally discuss faith as a separate topic (as with honesty, courage, etc.), no one (except Paul) *ever* states that salvation can occur with any of these virtues *apart from* works/deeds actions. This does not mean that, in *teaching* us the *behavior* of salvation that Jesus did not thus give us a free gift far beyond what we could ever earn, a gift of grace, but it does not mean that it was given entirely apart from specified behavioral conditions, as Paul says.

Occasionally, someone will bring up the case of the thief being crucified alongside Jesus, and note that Jesus said to him in Luke 23:43, "Today you will be with me in Paradise."

The claim is that Jesus granted salvation solely on his profession of support for the dying Jesus. However, we do not know what past aspects of character or behavior Jesus took into consideration that preceded the cross. Perhaps if one is hanging on a cross, the utterance of a word of encouragement to one in similar straits — truly humbled to the status of "least of these" — might be the most you can do. But again, we don't know why the thief was on the cross. Perhaps he had gotten caught stealing a loaf of bread from a Roman Centurion who had taken it from an impoverished widow, and the "thief" was trying to return it to its rightful owner. The text does not say, so I draw no conclusions, as are those who are quick to jump to conclusions about details not in the passage.

In any case, even if one accepted such an interpretation, it would simply be yet another Bible contradiction in addition to those already provided, since it directly opposes those verses I have cited in which Jesus clearly states that salvation is based on universal compassionate love expressed actively in deeds, but without mentioning faith or belief at all.

All of the gospels are replete with statements of behavioral obligation that *never* once make any statement remotely similar to Paul that the faith and grace that engender salvation occur "apart from" obedience, works or deeds.

Paul vs. James

Paul teaches that the gift of salvation through grace occurs apart from any behavioral requirement: Romans 3:28: "Therefore we conclude that a man is justified by faith *without the deeds of the law."*

Paul reiterates this position in: Romans 4:6; Galatians 2:16; Ephesians 2:8-9; II Timothy 1:9; Titus 3:5 — the first Bible writer to make the claim that salvation occurs apart from actions, which Paul repeatedly emphasizes.

Paul is specifically rebutted by the later writing of James (brother of Jesus) who offers one of the most striking and dramatic direct contradictions, in James 2:24, choosing vocabulary and syntax that specifically contradicts Paul's wording in Romans 3:28 in both content and construction:

Here are the two passages, shown in various translations:

Romans 3:28 (Paul)
> KJV: a man is *justified* by *faith* apart from *works* of the law.
> RSV: a man is *justified* by *faith* without the *deeds* of the law.
> Today's English Version: a person is *put right with god* only through *faith*, and not by *doing* what the Law commands.
> NIV: a man is *justified* by *faith* apart from *observing the law*.

James 2:24 (James' rebuttal)
> KJV: by *works* a man is *justified,* and not by *faith* only.
> RSV: a man is *justified* by *works* and not by *faith* alone.
> Today's English Version: it is by his *actions* that a person is *put right with god,* and not by his *faith* alone.
> NIV: a person is *justified* by what he *does* and not by *faith* alone.

Clearly, James seems to be saying exactly the opposite of what Paul says. The key words here, in both passages, are *justified* (or, in Today's English, "put right with God"), *works/deeds/actions* (or, in NIV, "observing the law"), and *faith* (same in all versions of both passages). Not only does James echo the same words, in the same parallel structure, but he even cites exactly the same example and scriptural reference! The passage from Paul comes near the end of the third chapter of Romans; immediately after that, opening up the fourth chapter, Paul cites the example of Abraham, and quotes from Genesis 15:6, and says it was Abrham's faith, not his works, that justified him (Romans 4:1-3). In James 2:21-24 (the same passage noted above), Paul's very example and scriptural reference are used against him, but with the opposite (and contradictory) conclusion, that Abraham was justified by the combination of faith with works. James' use of the same examples, quotes from the same Old Testament verse (Gen. 15:6) using the same words, and parallel structure clearly suggest that this was an intentional reply/rebuttal to Paul.

Examining the original texts: If anyone wants to suggest that, perhaps, the two passages have different root words in the original texts that just happened to pick up similar English equivalents by all these translators, then maybe we should look at the Greek source texts.

> The same Greek word ***dikaioo*** is used by *both* Paul AND James for the term justification (or "put right with God") in *both* passages. While the Today's English Version does use a different term in their English translation, at least they apply it consistently in both Romans and James.
>
> The same Greek word ***ergon*** is used by *both* Paul *and* James for the term variously translated as works, deeds, actions or "doing." While English translators haven't agreed on the best term, both Paul and James were talking about the same thing. And, with the exception of the NIV, the translators of

each version at least are consistent in their own usages between Paul and James. I wonder, however, about the objectivity of the NIV — one of the most popular texts among conservative Christians — in choosing to change the wording used between Paul and James in a way that subtly changes the connotation of Paul to be less in contradiction to James.

The same Greek word *pistis* is used by *both* Paul *and* James for the word that all versions of both passages translated as "faith." James is clearly rebutting Paul's scandalous undermining of Jesus' teachings.

Differences? Some have tried to explain these differences by saying that Paul and James had different meanings for their words "justification," "faith" and "works/deeds." Yet the simple fact remains they used the same words, in the same order and same context, even illustrated with the same example of Abraham and Isaac and the same scriptural citation from Genesis 15:6 (in reference to content; chapter and verse divisions had not yet been compiled).

On several occasions, attention has been called to one difference in the wording of Paul and James. While they use the same words, in the same context and the same order, when talking about the "works/deeds" Paul adds the phrase "of the law" while James does not. Some have argued that this means Paul is talking about something different. Not so.

Paul's use of that phrase is a restrictive modifying clause to limit the scope of his reference. By omitting it, James at the very least accepts everything in Paul's more restrictive context, broadened to include additional contexts. But earlier in the same chapter (James 2), just before the verse in question and his reference to Paul's example of Abraham and Isaac, James discusses behavior (2:8-13) in very specific in terms of deeds *of the Law*. Aside from the possibility of simply broadening the more narrow focus of Paul, what seems more likely *in context* is that James does not need to say "of the law" since he has already made it clear a few verses before that he is talking about "deeds of the law."

The only credible scenario is that James is clearly rebutting Paul's opposition to Jesus' teachings. Paul is not only rebutted by James in the examples above, but also admits having some problems getting along with Peter, admitting in Galatians 2:11: "But when Peter was come to Antioch, I withstood him to the face, because he was to be blamed."

In stark contrast to Paul's teaching of salvation by faith *apart from* behavioral manifestations, Jesus (Matt. 7:21-27), states unequivocally that the mere profession of accepting him is not enough, but that such a profession *must be* backed up by deeds. Jesus teaches a salvation of universal compassionate love expressed in *action.* It is the centerpiece of everything he taught. And Jesus himself consistently expressed love and closeness to sinners, lepers, tax collectors and other outcasts, while saving his rare words of harshness and anger for the Pharisees and Sadducees — the pompous, self-righteous elite of the established religious orthodoxy.

But what about when Paul also writes of compassion? Yes, it is true that there are a number of passages from Paul in praise of universal compassionate love expressed actively through deeds and, of course, these do not contradict Jesus. In particular, I Corinthians 13 is one of the most inspirational passages on charitable compassionate (agape) love in all of literature. I have quoted it often, and have cited it to show that, while Paul contradicts Jesus repeatedly, he does not always contradict Jesus on everything, and it has never been my position that he did.

Jesus and Paul agreed on quite a few things: the sun rises in the east; breathing air is good for humans, and compassionate love expressed in deeds is good.

But here is the contradictory difference on that last one, which is especially amplified by Jesus' brother James' stunningly direct rebuttal against Paul in James chapter 2:

Jesus (and James) state that both *faith* and *compassionate deeds* are good, but that *compassionate deeds are what get you into heaven* (but faith is good because it motivates you to do the good deeds, but is not absolutely mandatory).

Paul states that both *faith* and *compassionate deeds* are good, but that *faith is what gets you into heaven* (but compassionate deeds are good because they are a reflection of the sincerity of faith, but not absolutely mandatory).

The Law of Moses

Jesus was a Jewish rabbi who always upheld the Law of Moses. In his first public teaching, the Sermon on the Mount, he made it very clear in Matt. 5:18-19: "For verily I say unto you, Till heaven and earth pass, one jot or one tittle shall in no wise pass from the law, till all be fulfilled. Whosoever therefore shall break one of these least commandments, and shall teach men so, he shall be called the least in the kingdom of heaven: but whosoever shall do and teach [them], the same shall be called great in the kingdom of heaven." ("jot or tittle" in modern translations is "not one iota nor one dot".) Have heaven and earth passed away? Have *all* the prophecies, including those of the last days, been fulfilled?

Even some of the occasions when Jesus seems to add to the Law or teach in new and different ways, he goes to great lengths to show that it is based on the Law. For example, when this rabbi asked by a "lawyer" (one versed in the Law of Moses) what was the greatest commandment in the Law, Jesus turns the question back to him and asks what is in the Law, and from that extrapolates his great commandments to

Love God (from Deut 6:5) and Love Neighbor as Self (from Lev. 19:18) which was clearly the centerpiece of his ministry and his doctrine of *active* love and compassion for all.

Paul, on the other hand, wants to throw out the Law of Moses! Romans 3:19-21: "Now we know that what things soever the law saith, it saith to them who are under the law: that every mouth may be stopped, and all the world may become guilty before God. Therefore by the deeds of the law there shall no flesh be justified in his sight: for by the law [is] the knowledge of sin. But now the righteousness of God *without the law* is manifested, being witnessed by the law and the prophets." [Emphasis added]

And even more explicitly, Paul states in Romans 6:14, that "sin shall not have dominion over you: for *ye are not under the law,* but under grace."

Additionally, when Paul denounces the need for compassionate actions, or which Jesus and others spoke so much, in Romans 3:27-28 and Galatians 2:16, he also specifically mentions which works: that obedience to the Law is what is not required, contrary to Jesus' statements.

Other Problems with Paul

Manner of Worship: Jesus and Paul left contradictory legacies as to the manner in which worship should be conducted.

Jesus preached as an itinerant wanderer, informally to locals he encountered in his travels. Usually these were small groups, though he did encounter the occasional large crowd. Jesus always prayed privately, and taught his followers to do the same. In fact, he specifically prohibited public prayer and public displays of worship (Matt. 6:1-18). In fact, in verses 5 and 6, Jesus explicitly states, "when thou prayest, *thou shalt not...*" do so publicly in the synagogues or on the street corners. The fact that he belabored this point so thoroughly in his Sermon on the Mount, his first and greatest public teaching, almost suggest a premonition that others would follow to undermine and contradict him. Jesus did not organize any great church. He led a small, itinerant band of traveling wanderers from town to town. The closest he came to establishing any kind of authority was in Matt. 16:18, when he designated an itinerant fisherman named Simon to become "Peter" the "rock" upon which his church would be founded.

Paul, in contrast, organized a great system of churches. The story of Acts is the story of Paul traveling throughout the known world, establishing great churches. His epistles, which comprise the greatest single portion of the New Testament, about a third of it, were written to maintain administrative control of this great ecclesiastical network and to standardize its doctrines, not based on the teachings of Jesus, but on his own contradictory theology.

As with so many other issues, today's modern evangelical Christians fight for their right to expropriate public facilities for their worship and offer great churches with elaborate public worship rituals, once again coming down on the side of Paul and repudiating the simple teachings of the founder they accept, once again, in name only.

Dealing with sinners: Jesus ministered to the sinners, with no reluctance to engage adulterers, prostitutes, publicans, tax collectors, lepers, or any other "unclean" person (the whole need not a physician; a church is a hospital for sinners rather than a showcase for saints). This, of course, completely devastates the argument that god cannot be in the presence of sin by anyone who believes Jesus was god. Paul contradicts Jesus in 1Cor 5:11: "But now I have written unto you not to keep company, if any man that is called a brother be a

Paul vs. Jesus

fornicator, or covetous, or an idolater, or a railer, or a drunkard, or an extortioner; with such an one no not to eat."

Feeding the poor: Jesus taught in Matt 25:31-46 that our final salvation and judgment would be based in large part on our willingness to feed the poor. Jesus further emphasizes the importance of feeding the poor, apart from salvation issues, repeatedly throughout his ministry (Matt 19:21; Matt: 25:31-46; Matt 26:9; Mark 10:21; Luke 18:22; John 12:6). Jesus never, not once, imposes any qualification or conditional limitation on this requirement. Paul contradicts this: 2Thess 3:10 "For even when we were with you, this we commanded you, that if any would not work, neither should he eat." Does this mean that if poor people are unemployed, we should turn them away from any charity?

Slavery: When the Southerners in our country sought to defend slavery, they called upon Paul to back them up, citing Ephesians 6:5 and Titus 2:9-10, in which Paul exhorts slaves to obey their masters, yet Paul never even once condemned this evil that was so widely practiced in his time. Here, Paul again contradicts Jesus, who exalted the "least of these" (Matt 25:31-46) and elevated the servants above masters (Matt 20:27 and 23:11; and Mark 9:35 & 10:44).

Equality for Women: Paul was very anti-woman. He ordered that they not be allowed to speak in the churches (1Cor 14:34-45) and that they stay home and take care of the kids (1Timothy 2:12; 5:14), and that wives should be submissive to the mastery of their husbands (Ephesians 5:22-24 and Colossians 3:18-19).

This, of course, is in direct opposition to Jesus, who elevated women — even women of lowly status such as prostitutes, Samaritans (woman by the well), and everyday women such as Mary and Martha — to a degree unprecedented for that time. Note that in Luke 10:38-42, Jesus even chastises Martha for accepting a traditional woman's role, while he praises her sister Mary for choosing the "better part" of more active participation. This was obviously recognized by the women of that time, as Luke 8:2-3 lists the names of a number of prominent women of means who provided economic support for Jesus' ministry.

Homosexuals: The *only* passage in the New Testament offered as evidence against equal rights for homosexuals is from Paul (Romans 1:24-27). Jesus himself never uttered a single word against ` relationships and, given his affinity for sinners, lepers, tax collectors, and other outcasts (the "least of these"), it is likely that in our modern times it would be Jesus who would be embracing the homosexuals rejected by those who claim to be his followers. Just as it was Paul's words that were held up in the mid-1800's to justify slavery, so Paul's words today are still used to persecute others.

There has been a popular piece that has been circulated among many Christian churches and publications, using a description of Paul and his background (without identifying him) on a résumé applying for a position as a pastor and ask if you would hire him. After turning him down, the punch line is that, just knowing data and not identity, you have just rejected the Apostle Paul. The message is supposed to be about judging others but, there is another message: knowing what we *do* know about Paul, *many* Christians are inclined to find him rather unsavory. Those who claim to take upon them the name of **Jesus** should carefully examine Paul's undermining of Jesus' message and his many contradictions of Jesus and the other apostles, as well as the plain nonsense of his bloody atonement theory of human sacrifice, and then decide if they want to be Christians or Paulians.

Punishment for Adam's sin

Paul is the one who introduces the concept of original sin and the "inheritance" of sin, in Romans 5:12, "Wherefore, as by one man sin entered into the world, and death by sin, and so death passed upon all men, for that all have sinned."

Why are we, in any way whatsoever, held "responsible" for the sins of Adam and Eve? How can a person be "guilty" of something they didn't do, which in fact was done thousands of years before they were even conceived? How can there be an "inherited" moral flaw. Morality is a matter of "right and wrong," not a physical, tangible object. In any case, how can you be responsible for something you had nothing to do with?

If my father and mother do something wrong, why do I get punished for that? What do *their* wrongs have to do with *my* sins? Talk about unfair!

I cannot imagine that a god could be called "just" who allows people to be punished for something they have no control over: the way they were born; i.e., the way god created them. Is sin a matter of moral character, or a birth defect? Should babies born with birth defects be punished? Should we require abortions for fetuses born deformed?

It is interesting to note that while Paul invents a theology of atonement based on the offering of Jesus as a human sacrifice for sin, Jesus explicitly rejects this doctrine. The gospel according to Matthew *twice,* in Matt 9:13 and Matt 12:7, states that Jesus said: "I will have mercy, and not sacrifice" (KJV). More modern translations, such as the RSV and NIV, update the archaic meaning of the word "will" and translate Jesus' statements in both verses as: "I *desire* mercy and not sacrifice" (emphasis added). This could not be a more explicit rejection of Paul's later teaching.

Betrayal of Jesus

Why Do People Follow Paul?

I have been asked occasionally why I believe so many people are willing to follow Paul. My thoughts boil down to basically two reasons:

1. It is the easy way. Jesus requires you to actually transform your character and put it into action. Paul says, "Just have faith and believe" and you get a free gift, without ever having to actually DO anything — something for nothing; the easy way out; the lazy man's way to salvation; the free ride.

2. As has been noted previously, Paul was wealthy, educated, and had the rare status of being both a Jew and a Roman citizen, affording him both the means and papers with which to travel. He was able to travel widely, throughout the entire Roman empire, converting gullible victims by the thousands, giving him extraordinary power, and all of them had their interpretation of what Jesus taught coming by way of Paul's version, so it gained traction early.

The doctrine of salvation by atonement through the bloody human sacrifice of a sinless substitute originates from Paul. It is fundamentally contradictory to the key principles taught by Jesus and his brother, James, yet it has become the core principle upon which evangelical Christian theology is founded. This doctrine has its own logical flaws and errors and merits further in-depth analysis and scrutiny:

5

Bloody Human Sacrifice Atonement Mythology

One of the central foundations upon which most Christian religions are centered is the doctrine that Jesus died on the Cross in an atoning sacrifice that "paid the price for" our sins which then allows us to be eligible for Eternal Salvation.

The specific details of how this works vary from Catholics to evangelical Christians to Mormons and to other sects of Christianity, but for the most part, other than the most liberal of denominations which take a less doctrinaire view of the subject, most Christians teach this belief at their core.

An important question at the core of this belief in an atoning sacrifice would be: what is required for mortal humans to enter "heaven" or "paradise" in whatever life exists after death. Central to that is the role of Jesus in that

Betrayal of Jesus

"salvation": does he offer us the path to Salvation because he taught us the path we should follow, or because he died for our sins in an Atonement?

Whether or not there is any life after this one, it could be clearly argued that the moral teachings of Jesus, centered on universal compassion expressed in behavioral action, at least make the world a better place in this life. If there is life after this one and his teachings continue to better our existence after death, so much the better. There is much to be said for what Jesus reportedly taught his followers and, through the record that has been handed down, to us.

Yet there are many who would undermine this legacy, and weaken it with a bloody mythology of human sacrifice. They would simplistically dismiss Jesus' teachings about the need for behavioral action, and preach that salvation exists because Jesus died on a cross as payment for our sins. Such a belief shows a total disregard for human accountability in achieving salvation, and allows someone like Beverly Russell [stepfather to Susan Smith (who drowned her two innocent boys)], to molest his daughter over a period of years — as a teenager and even continuing as a young married mother — and, by becoming a "born-again believer" receive complete forgiveness, without any other real change of character or behavior. No wonder he joined the Christian Coalition! Is this a great religion, or what!?

Focus On Greed

The emphasis of the belief in bloody human sacrifice mythology is one of greed: getting a "free gift" for doing nothing in exchange. This, of course, contrasts directly with the teaching of Jesus to love others and *give* unselfishly, as Jesus is quoted in Acts 20:35 as having said, "It is more blessed to give than

Bloody Human Sacrifice Atonement

to receive." How different from the focus on *getting* a free gift, which is the emphasis of atonement mentality.

Sinners in the Presence of God

First of all, the need for an Atonement seems to hinge on the concept that our "sins" must somehow be "washed away," owing to a concept that no "unclean" thing (or person) can tolerate the presence of a perfect god, and thus there is the need for a mediator to cleanse such "unclean" mortal sinners.

Yet, while the worshippers of bloody human sacrifice mythology would have us believe that it is predicated on the fact that god cannot have imperfect sinners in his presence, these same people believe that this same god (incarnate as Jesus) embraced the lowliest and most sinful and sought them in his presence! One cannot logically believe that Jesus was God, that God cannot abide the presence of sinners, and that Jesus embraced, touched and love sinners in his presence.

The scenario goes something like this: "I need to be pure or of perfect goodness in order to enter the kingdom of god. But I am blemished with sin, a stain that I am incapable of washing out myself. My lack of goodness constitutes a debt, but lacking the requisite goodness, I am not able to pay this debt myself." Therefore, I need someone perfect (of enough pure goodness) who has the capacity, or richness, or affordability to pay the debt on my behalf." Thus, the need of a savior or mediator.

Need for a Mediator?

It seems to me that this presents a very wimpy view of what is supposed to be an omnipotent, all-powerful deity. Either he/she is incapable of withstanding the presence of one "tainted" with "sin" (is this weak or what?), or is incapable

Betrayal of Jesus

on creating the right times and situations where one so tainted might be able to approach his/her divine presence. Both are limitations on the "power" of the "all"-mighty. [Compare Romans 8:38-39: Neither death nor life, neither angels nor demons, neither the present nor the future, nor any powers, neither height nor depth, nor anything else in all creation, will be able to separate us from the love of God that is Jesus Christ our Lord.]

If god is our spiritual father, then shouldn't he at least measure up to the standards of imperfect, puny mortal fathers? (See Matt 7:11). I am a "Daddy" as well as a "Grandpa." If my daughter or granddaughter did something wrong, or got "dirty," I would still have the ability (as weak and imperfect as I am compared to a god) to stoop to her level, hold her close to me and try to help her through the problem. Her imperfection, even if it required some form of punishment or discipline, would not prevent me from being able to remain close to her, if I really loved her. It might require some form of remedial attention, but that would not necessarily mean separation. So how can some people claim that a god described as being all powerful can't even remain close to his spiritual children if that's what he wants? Why are they imposing limits on what god can or can't do? Is he all powerful or isn't he? Why does he need a mediator? And if Jesus is really god, and they are one and the same, then he isn't really an intercessor or mediator at all — he would be interceding to or mediating with *himself!*

And even if the whole ludicrous concept made any sense at all, we still wouldn't need a Messiah. If a perfect being needed to "take upon himself" the sins of others, why couldn't god just do it himself? If Jesus, assuming the debt, has the right to forgive it, why doesn't the original debtholder? Why not just be efficient and cut out the middleman (which is, literally, what the "mediator" is)? Why can this omnipotent deity forgive *after* being crucified but not *before?* How does Jesus' torture give an omnipotent God more power to forgive than he already had? And, if one holds a concept of trinity, which says that Jesus IS god, then, in fact, there IS no mediator or middleman anyway, god is just punishing *himself,* so what exactly is the point? What is accomplished?

Suffering for all the sins of humankind

The concept of atonement often includes the belief that Jesus also took upon himself the suffering for all the sins of all persons who have ever lived, now live or will ever live.

Even if you believe that Jesus somehow took upon himself that suffering, as well as the suffering of every other sin against every other human who ever lived or will live, I have never even heard anyone even suggest that Jesus' "taking upon him the suffering for those sins" in any way also took away the suffering of those victims. At the very best, if you can even believe that he did that, all you have is a single instance in which you simply double the amount of suffering in the universe (once by the victim and again by Jesus when he re-experiences all this suffering). You have not taken away the victimhood of the original victim. If Jesus could take away the pain and suffering of those victims, and transfer the entire victimhood away from them and solely to himself, this concept might hold a little more merit. But we all know that didn't happen. No one has ever even claimed that all the victims were relieved of their suffering, since everyone of us has endured some level of suffering for others' sins against us so we all know that it didn't happen. If Jesus just added another instance of that suffering to himself, then all you have is an increase of suffering, and for what? Sorry, but

Betrayal of Jesus

I just can't see an all-knowing, all-wise deity working that way. Let's imagine the worst possible crime: an evil, malicious man kidnaps, molests, tortures and ultimately murders an innocent young child. The child suffers terribly through every phase of this crime. The fact that Jesus died on the cross or even re-experienced all that suffering does not undo or eliminate the fact of how much this child has suffered. Even a smaller crime, like schoolyard bullying or taunting someone who is "different" — the victim has suffered, and Jesus' death did nothing to change that.

Paying "The Price"

If Jesus "paid" a "ransom" for our sins, *who did he pay it to?* Is it to the Devil, who owns our souls because we are imprisoned in sin (Satan has "kidnapped" our souls) — would God pay off a ransom to a criminal? Or does Jesus pay this "ransom" to God — the supreme judge of the eternal court? Does God extort the payment of ransoms like a common kidnapper? If Jesus is God, is he paying the ransom to himself?

Secondly, *did he pay* the ransom? The Bible says "The wages of sin is death" [Romans 6:23 (as part of Paul's ridiculous atonement theory based on a transferably physical concept of sin that goes way beyond the purely symbolic gestures of animal sacrifices or scapegoats in the Old Testament in Lev 16:9-10)]. The consequence of sin is HELL [Matt 5:22, 29, 30; 10:28; 18:9; Mk 9:43, 47; Rev 20:14-15 and many more]. Did Jesus die? Well, he was killed on the cross. But, in that sense, *all* humans die — so, if that is what pays the price of sin, we *all* pay for our sins, so why do we need a surrogate to pay it for us? If something on the order of 36 hours worth of being "dead" (from sunset Friday to sunrise Sunday — notwithstanding that Matt 12:40 and Mark 8:31

Bloody Human Sacrifice Atonement

prophecy that the "son of man" will stay buried *three days and three nights* — more contradictions and failed prophecies) pays the price of all sins of all persons who ever lived, now live, or will ever live, then if each person pays their own share, stays dead for a brief time, then why can't they then live in heaven, having paid their price? Since your belief is that those who don't accept Jesus WILL pay their own price (to satisfy justice if they reject mercy), then they must be capable of paying it. So let them pay it, come back from their sleep, and let eternal life roll forward!

Did Jesus die in some other sense? Is he dead? No! Christians tell us that *he lives!* He is *not dead,* and he is *not in hell* — he is at the *right hand of god!* He did *not* pay the price that we would have had to pay without his supposed sacrifice.

Sin Transference

Part of the problem with the concept of blood atonement, beyond the need for absolutely purity already discussed, is that it does not address the nature of sin — what "sin" is — and thus how to become cleansed from it. "Sin" is not a tangible, physical object, like a ball or a Frisbee, that you can throw or catch or hold onto or give from one person to another. Sin is an intangible function of character, representing the negative aspects of character flaws just as virtue represents the positive aspects of character goodness. While one might use allegoric examples from the physical world to illustrate ideas, the literal belief that you can transfer sin from one person (the sinner) to another (a guiltless substitute) is absurd because it contravenes the very nature of sin. And, in fact, the absurdity of saying that Jesus took upon himself all the suffering for sin is made clear by the fact that, as a consequence of mortals' sins, the original participants (both perpetrators and victims) did *not* have their suffering transferred to

Jesus. They still suffered fully, so if Jesus also suffered, the only thing that happened was a doubling of the suffering, which hardly seems to be an act of either justice or mercy. Killing Jesus did not undo the original sins he supposedly took upon himself or the suffering that resulted from them.

While the Old Testament clearly has symbolic gestures of sin transference such as animal sacrifices (detailed in the first and third chapters of Leviticus and numerous other references) and the infamous "scapegoat,"* Paul is the one who seems to have adapted this to a literal transference with a human sacrifice. While Jesus does mention ransom for sin and forgiveness for sin (and please note that words such as "ransom" or "sacrifice" do not imply sin transference — those who pay ransoms to kidnappers do not transfer sins, and heroes who give their lives for others do not take upon themselves the sins of those others), Paul is the one who introduces a literal concept of sin transference.

Additionally, Paul is the *only* one, directly contradicting numerous other New Testament references, who says that this atonement occurs completely *apart from* the requirement of any behavioral component (works or deeds). Many Bible teachers, including Jesus himself, do emphasize the need for faith — but always in conjunction with the ensuing behavioral action which follows. Paul stands alone in teaching that faith can exist *apart from* behavioral response or character transformation.

---

* The scapegoat reference in Leviticus 16:9-10 clearly does not refer to Jesus. Jesus was always referred to as the "lamb of God," not the "goat" of God. Jesus repeatedly makes a big distinction between lambs (or sheep) and goats (read Matt 25:31-45). Lambs represent salvation; goats represent damnation. In any case, the scapegoat is purely symbolic and does not represent at all a literal teaching of sin transference. Today the concept of a "scapegoat" is ridiculed as an example of injustice.

Punished for OTHERS' sins?

Furthermore, Paul not only teaches a ridiculous concept of sin transference in regard to expunging our *own* sins, but he goes even further with suggestions in Romans 5:14 and I Cor 15:22 that many have interpreted to mean that we also have to be redeemed from the transgressions (sins) of Adam and Eve! If my father and mother do something wrong, why should I get punished for that — something that happened before I was even born? What do *their* wrongs have to do with *my* sins? Talk about unfair! The scenario is ridiculous enough if the atonement supposedly pays a physical price (transferable, with no explanation of how) for my *own* sins. When Paul suggests that it isn't even for *my* sins, but for someone else's, he has really lost any semblance of justice!

There is no logical connection between killing an innocent man and making the sins of others go away! The only purpose served by this bloodthirsty doctrine of human sacrifice is to propose an easier way, based on affinity or loyalty — us vs. them — instead of actually having to change your flawed character and then live by what you profess. It transforms Christianity from a movement of activists reaching out to those in need, into a movement of subservient followers. The entire doctrine of blood atonement to take away sins is not merely irrational, but a device invented by the renegade "apostle" Paul for bypassing the much higher standard for salvation taught by Jesus himself — that salvation can only occur through universal compassionate love expressed actively in deeds.

Civil or Criminal?

Even the analogy of "paying the debt" is inappropriate. It would be more applicable to a civil debt, whereas the commission of sin is more akin to a criminal violation. While we

Betrayal of Jesus

might appreciate that one person can pay the debt of another, we would not tolerate innocent people being punished for guilty ones. If a convicted serial murder/rapist plead guilty to multiple counts of murder and rape, would we allow his law-abiding gray-haired mother to volunteer to step in and serve his prison time (or be executed) in his stead? Following that "satisfaction of justice," would we then tolerate allowing the murder/rapist to be turned back onto the streets?

Jesus' Gift of Salvation

What, then, *is* the role of Jesus in salvation (either in a life after this one or in making this one a happier and more peaceful existence)?

First of all, Jesus explicitly and emphatically rejects Paul's teaching, referenced in the preceding paragraphs, of a salvation theology based on atonement through a bloody human sacrifice. The gospel according to Matthew *twice,* in Matt 9:13 and Matt 12:7, states that Jesus said: "I will have mercy, and not sacrifice" (King James Version). More modern translations, such as the Revised Standard Version and New International Version, update the archaic meaning of the word "will" and translate Jesus' statements in both verses as: "I *desire* mercy and not sacrifice" (emphasis added). This could not be a more explicit rejection of Paul's later teaching.

A loving but omnipotent god would have the ability to condescend to the level of imperfect sinners and make them feel comfortable in his presence. In our modern world, highly educated medical professional go into emergency rooms to care for those covered with blood and dirt or risk their lives ("greater love hath no man") in the presence of those with deadly incurable communicable diseases; counselors work with those who are poor, in jail, or abused to help them find a

Bloody Human Sacrifice Atonement

better way; and teachers condescend to the level of those who are uneducated to lead them out of ignorance. 2,000 years ago, Jesus (reputed to be perfect and a representative of the Godhead) made those who were dirty, poor and reviled to feel comfortable in his presence. He touched lepers, forgave sinners, blessed the poor and consorted with (yuck!) tax collectors. As has been previously noted in earlier chapters, it was the central message from Jesus: his first teaching, his last teaching and the foundation of his teaching in between.

At the beginning of his ministry, Jesus taught us to love our enemies. Later, when asked by a lawyer what is the "greatest commandment" in the law, this Jewish rabbi quoted from the Old Testament law to love god [Deut 6:5] and love your neighbor as yourself [Lev 19:18], as reported in Luke 10:25-37 and Matt 22:36-40. Note further, that in the Luke account, this was illustrated by an example, the parable of the Good Samaritan, which was used to define "neighbor" very broadly, to include enemies. The Samaritan (the hated enemy) is the one who exemplifies this broad definition, and who provides the example of one who is saved by their compassionate actions toward their enemy. Yet the Samaritan is not even a believer, not one having "faith" nor one who has accepted Jesus as savior, yet this is who Jesus chooses as the example of one who gains eternal life, which is what the lawyer specifically asked.

In his *last* general teaching, Jesus said that salvation would be based on our love for god in how we treat those whom he called "the least of these" (Matt 25:31-46). In his own actions, Jesus consistently expressed love and closeness to sinners, lepers, tax collectors and other outcasts, while saving his rare words of harshness and anger for the Pharisees and Sadducees — the pompous, self-righteous administrators of the established religious orthodoxy.

Yet some would assert this ridiculous doctrine that god is incapable of adhering to this doctrine, because either he/she cannot withstand the presence of these least ones, or is incapable of making them feel comfortable in his/her presence. What kind of eternal parent is incapable of embracing his/her weak, imperfect children, even when they are dirty or hurting and need that presence the most?

The Real Process of Removing Stains

But, even if such a scenario were correct — that we must have all "stains" removed before we can be in the presence of god — (only for the sake of argument, since I do *not* agree, as noted previously), the process of using a "mediator" to eliminate the stain of those sins by "paying off a debt" is terribly simplistic and flawed. It does not address the real nature of sin. It treats good and evil as physical commodities — something tangible, like a baseball or a Frisbee that you can chase and catch, as previously discussed.

Aside from the problem with why we cannot simply cleanse the stain ourselves with a good washing (learning correct principles and values to offset the wrong ones), or go out and productively *earn* enough "goodness currency" to pay the debt off ourselves, it does not address the nature of sin and of how to overcome it.

Sin is a negative spiritual essence — a flaw of character — *not* a tangible object. It exists as a negative form of consciousness, of thought, of motive, of spirit — in some way that intangible energy of life force in its negative expression.

It is not an object that can be bought, sold, lent, owed, or the object of indebtedness. If I am burdened by sin, there is no physical action that another person can take to remove it. The only thing another person can do is reach me at the

Bloody Human Sacrifice Atonement

applicable level of consciousness, of thought, of motive, or spirit involved — by condescending to my sinful level, if necessary and teaching me what is right, or developing in me right values, attitudes, feelings and motives that will lead to changed feelings and a new life.

The atonement concept represents the same mentality as the misguided people who seek happiness (which is also not physical in nature) so they try to pursue it directly, by selfish means, as if they could reach out and grab it like chasing a baseball or a butterfly, instead of setting in motion the internal processes which allow happiness to develop naturally. In the same way, overcoming "sin" or evil is an internal transformational process, not something that can be handed off to someone else.

Punishment or payment are not part of the equation, except insofar as they may help in an instructive manner. And especially there is no logical need for punishing an innocent man for the sins of others. What a miscarriage of justice! Even if Jesus' sacrifice were voluntary, or a noble gesture of love on his part, it would be a manifestation of *his* goodness; it would do nothing for *our* salvation. There is simply *no logical connection* between an innocent man hanging painfully on an old wooden cross, and the eradication of evil thoughts, motives, or behavior from those who can only do so through a change of heart and attitude through the experience of kindness, love and compassionate joy.

The irony is that Jesus, in what he taught throughout his ministry — not in an "atonement," but in a consistent message of universal compassion actively expressed — provided the means for character reformation and grown that actually can transform the sinner and allow him to overcome sin. By developing feelings of universal compassion and then expressing them in action, or if one does not feel such feelings, do the actions anyway until they become natural to you and you do feel the compassion, character is truly transformed. Those who are hardened become softened and gentle. Character is transformed. Sin is expunged.

Yet Jesus is remembered and worshipped as a savior for his suffering and death on the cross, and supposed resurrection, which became an "atonement" for sin. In cruel irony, this off-centered emphasis, founded in greedy motives of selfishness, along with a preoccupation on rituals, ceremonies and unrelated lesser teachings, distract most of Jesus' nominal followers from primary attention on the core of what he actually taught.

6
Additional Contradictions

In the preceding chapter on the false doctrine of Bible worship, I present a number of contradictions and flaws to establish my point that, while the Bible is of great moral and historical importance, it is by no means inerrant or infallible. In the chapter, I cite just a few key contradictions to make my point.

In fact, there are hundreds more. The ones I cited in the body of the book were some that were major contradictions on key issues. Of the hundreds of additional contradictions, some are on key points, others on trivial details. Regardless, a single valid contradiction or error is sufficient to prove fallibility of the Bible.

Following is an additional list of contradictions, many of which are trivial but still demonstrate Biblical fallibility. They can also be found online at
http://www.wordwiz72.com/contr.txt

BETRAYAL OF JESUS

Additional Contradictions:

God is satisfied / dissatisfied with his works.
Gen 1:31 / Gen 6:6

God dwells / dwells not in chosen temples.
2 Chron 7:12,16 / Acts 7:48

If someone is not for God, he is against God; or if not against, then for.
Matt 12:30, Luke 11:23 / Mark 9:40, Luke 9:50.

God dwells in light / darkness.
1 Tim 6:16 / 1 Kings 8:12; Ps 18:11; Ps 97:2

God is seen and heard / invisible and cannot be heard.
Ex 33:23,11; Gen 3:9,10; Gen 32:30; Is 6:1; Ex 24:9-11 / John 1:18; John 5:37; Ex 33:20; 1 Tim 6:16

God is tired and rests / never tired and never rests.
Ex 31:17; Jer 15:6 / Is 40:28

God is everywhere present, sees and knows all things / not everywhere, neither sees nor knows all things.
Prov 15:3; Ps 139:7-10; Job 34:22,21 / Gen 11:5; Gen 18:20,21; Gen 3:8

God knows the hearts of men / tries men to find out.
Acts 1:24; Ps 139:2,3 / Deut 13:3, 8:2; Gen 22:12

God is / is not all powerful.
Jer 32:27; Mt 19:26 / Judg 1:19

God is unchangeable / changeable.
James 1:17; Mal 3:6; Ezek 24:14; Num 23:19 / Gen 6:6; Jonah 3:10; 1 Sam 2:30,31; 2 Kings 20:1,4-6; Ex 33:1,3,17,14

God is just and impartial / unjust and partial.
Ps 92:15; Gen 18:25; Deut 32:4; Rom 2:11; Ezek 18:25 / Gen 9:25; Ex 20:5; Rom 9:11-13; Mt 13:12

God is / is not the author of evil.
Lam 3:38; Jer 18:11; Is 45:7; Amos 3:6; Ezek 20:25 / 1 Cor 14:33; Deut 32:4; James 1:13

God gives freely to those who ask / withholds blessings.
James 1:5; Luke 11:10 / John 12:40; Josh 11:20; Is 63:17

God is warlike / peaceful.
Ex 15:3; Is 51:15 / Rom 15:33; 1 Cor 14:33

ADDITIONAL CONTRADICTIONS

God is cruel, unmerciful, destructive and ferocious / kind, merciful and good.
Num 31:1,17-18,42-47; Deut 4:24 ; Deut 7:16; Jer 13:14; 1 Sam 15:2-3; 1 Sam 6:19; / James 5:11; Lam 3:33; 1 Chron 16;34; Ezek 18:32; Ps 145:9; 1 Tim 2:4; 1 John 4:16; Ps 25:8

God's anger is fierce, endures long / is slow and ends quickly.
Num 32:13; Num 25:4; Jer 17:4 / Ps 103:8; Ps 30:5

God commands, approves of and delights in burnt offerings, sacrifices and holy days / disapproves of and has no pleasure in burnt offerings, sacrifices and holy days.
Ex 29:36; Lev 23:27; Ex 29:18; Lev 1:9 / Jer 7:22; Jer 6:20; Ps 50:13,14; Is 1:11-13

God accepts / forbids human sacrifices.
2 Sam 21:8,9,14; Gen 22:2; Judg 11:30-32,34,38,39 / Deut 12:30,31

God tempts man / tempts no man.
Gen 22:1; 2 Sam 24:1; Jer 20:7; Mt 6:13 / James 1:13

God cannot lie / God lies by proxy, sends lying spirits.
Heb 6:18 / 2 Thes 2:11; 1 Kings 22:23; Ezek 14:9

God destroys / will not destroy man because of wickedness.
Gen 6:5,7 / Gen 8:21

God's attributes are revealed in his works / attributes cannot be discovered.
Rom 1:20 / Job 11:7; Is 40:28

There is but one God / there is a plurality of gods.
Deut 6:4 / Gen 1:26; Gen 3:22; Gen 18:1-3; 1 John 5:7

Women can / cannot preach in the church
Romans 16:1-2 / 1 Cor 14:34-35

Robbery commanded / forbidden.
Ex 3:21,22; Ex 12:35,36 / Lev 19:13; Ex 20:15

Lying approved and sanctioned / forbidden.
Josh 2:4-6; James 2:25; Ex 1:18-20; 1 Kings 22:21,22 / Ex 20:16; Prov 12:22;
Rev 21:8

Hatred of the Edomite sanctioned / forbidden.
2 Kings 14:7,3 / Deut 23:7

Killing commanded / forbidden.
Ex 32:27 / Ex 20:13

Betrayal of Jesus

Blood shedder must die / must not die.
Gen 9:5,6 / Gen 4:15

Making of images forbidden / commanded.
Ex 20:4 / Ex 25:18,20

Slavery and oppression ordained / forbidden.
Gen 9:25-27; Lev 25:45,46; Joel 3:8 / Is 58:6; Ex 22:21; Ex 21:16; Mt 23:10

Improvidence enjoined / condemned.
Mt 6:28,31,34; Luke 6:30,35; Luke 12:3 / 1 Tim 5:8; Prov 13:22

Anger approved / disapproved.
Eph 4:26 / Eccl 7:9; Prov 22:24; James 1:20

Good works to be seen of men / not to be seen.
Mt 5:16 / Mt 6:1

Judging of others forbidden / approved.
Mt 7:1,2 / 1 Cor 6:2-4, 5:12

Jesus taught non-resistance / taught and practiced physical resistance.
Mt 5:39; Mt 26:52 / Luke 22:36; John 2:15

Jesus warned followers not to fear being killed / Jesus himself avoided being killed.
Luke 12:4 / John 7:1

Public prayer sanctioned / disapproved.
1 Kings 8:22,54; Kings 9:3 / Mt 6:5,6

Importunity in prayer commended / condemned.
Luke 18:5,7; Luke 11:8 / Mt 6:7,8

Wearing of long hair by men sanctioned / condemned.
Judg 13:5; Num 6:5 / 1 Cor 11:14

Circumcision instituted / condemned.
Gen 17:10 / Gal 5:2

The Sabbath instituted / repudiated.
Ex 20:8 / Is 1:13; Rom 14:5; Col 2:16

Creation / escape from Egypt reason for Sabbath.
Ex 20:11 / Deut 5:15

No work to be done on Sabbath under penalty of death / Jesus broke the Sabbath and justified disciples to do same.
Ex 31:15; Num 15:32,36 / John 5:16; Mt 12:1-3,5

Additional Contradictions

Baptism commanded / not commanded.
Mt 28:19 / 1 Cor 1:17,14

Every animal allowed for food / some animals prohibited.
Gen 9:3; 1 Cor 10:25; Rom 14:14 / Deut 14:7,8

Taking of oaths sanctioned / forbidden.
Num 30:2; Gen 21:23,24,31; Gen 31:53; Heb 6:13 / Mt 5:34

Marriage approved / disapproved.
Gen 2:18; Gen 1:28; Mt 19:5; Heb 13:4 / 1 Cor 7:1, 1 Cor 7:7,8

Freedom of divorce permitted / restricted.
Deut 24:1; Deut 21:10,11,14 / Mt 5:32

Adultery forbidden / allowed.
Ex 20:14; Heb 13:4 / Num 31:18; Hos 1:2; Hos 2:1-3

Marriage or cohabitation with a sister denounced / God blessed Abraham's marriage to sister.
Deut 27:22; Lev 20:17 / Gen 20:11,12; Gen 17:16

A man may / may not marry his brother's widow.
Deut 25:5 / Lev 20:21

Hatred to kindred enjoined / condemned.
Luke 14:26 / Eph 6:2; Eph 5:25,29; 1 John 3:15

Intoxicating beverages recommended / discountenanced.
Prov 31:6,7; 1 Tim 5:23; Ps 104:15 / Prov 20:1; Prov 23:31,32

It is our duty to obey our rulers, who are god's ministers and punish evil doers only / it is not our duty to always obey rulers who sometimes punish the good and receive unto themselves damnation therefor.
Rom 13:1-3,6; Mt 23:2,3; 1 Pet 2:13,14; Eccl 8:2,5 / Ex 1:17,20; Dan 3:16,18; Dan 6:9,7,10; Acts 4:26,27; Mark 12:38-40; Luke 23:11,24,33,35

Women's rights denied / affirmed.
Gen 3:16; 1 Tim 2:12; 1 Cor 14:34; 1 Pet 3:6 / Judg 4:4,14,15; Judg 5:7; Acts 2:18; Acts 21:9

Obedience to masters enjoined / obedience to God only.
Col 3:22,23; 1 Pet 2:18 / Mt 4:10; Mt 23:10; 1 Cor 7:23

There is / is no unpardonable sin.
Mark 3:29 / Acts 13:39

Man created before / after animals.
Gen 2:18,19 / Gen 1:25-27

Betrayal of Jesus

Planting and harvest always / ceased for seven years.
Gen 8:22 / Gen 41:54,56

Pharaoh's heart hardened by God / pharaoh.
Ex 4:21; Ex 9:12 / Ex 8:15

All / not all cattle, horses died.
Ex 9:3,6 / Ex 14:9

Moses feared / did not fear pharaoh.
Ex 2:14,15,23; Ex 4:19 / Heb 11:27

24,000 / 23,000 died in plague.
Num 25:9 / 1 Cor 10:8

John the Baptist was / was not Elijah.
Mt 11:14 / John 1:21

Joseph's father was Jacob / Heli.
Mt 1:16 / Luke 3:23

Salah's father was Arphaxad / Cainan.
Gen 11:12 / Luke 3:35,36

14 / 13 generations from Abraham to David.
Mt 1:17 / Mt 1:2-6

14 / 13 generations from captivity to Jesus.
Mt 1:17 / Mt 1:12-16

Infant Jesus taken / not taken to Egypt.
Mt 2:14,15,19,21,23 / Luke 2:22,39

Jesus was tempted / not tempted in the wilderness.
Mark 1:12,13 / John 2:1,2

Two different genealogies of Jesus.
Mt 1:1-17 / Luke 3:23-38

Jesus is / is not son of David.
Mt 1:1; Luke 1:32; Rom 1:3 / Mt 22:43-46; Mark 12:36,37

Risen Jesus says touch me / touch me not.
John 20:27 / John 20:17

Jesus preached first sermon on the mount / plain.
Mt 5:1,2 / Luke 6:17,20

John in / not in prison when Jesus went into Galilee.
Mark 1:14 / John 1:43; John 3:22-24

Disciples to go forth with / without staff and sandals.
Mark 6:8,9 / Mt 10:9,10

ADDITIONAL CONTRADICTIONS

Woman of Canaan / Greece besought Jesus.
Mt 15:22 / Mark 7:26

Two / one blind men besought Jesus.
Mt 20:30 / Luke 18:35,38

Jesus was crucified at the third / sixth hour.
Mark 15:25 / John 19:14,15

Two / one thieves reviled Jesus.
Mt 27:44; Mark 15:32 / Luke 23:39,40

Satan entered Judas at / before last supper.
John 13:27 / Luke 22:3,4,7

Judas hanged himself / died another way.
Mt 27:5 / Acts 1:18

Potter's field purchased by Judas / chief priests.
Acts 1:18 / Mt 27:6,7

One / two / three / more, women came to sepulchre.
John 20:1; Mt 28:1 / Mark 16:1; Luke 24:10

It was sunrise / before sunrise when they came to the sepulchre.
Mark 16:2 / John 20:1

Two angels standing / one angel sitting, at the sepulchre.
Luke 24:4 / Mt 28:2,5

Two / one angels in the sepulchre.
John 20:11,12 / Mark 16:5

Jesus was to be three / two days, nights in the grave.
Mt 12:40 / Mk 15:25,42,44-46; Mk 16:19

Holy ghost bestowed at / before Pentecost.
Acts 1:8,5; Acts 2:1,4 / John 20:22

Disciples to tarry in Jerusalem / go immediately to Galilee.
Mt 28:10 / Luke 24:49

Jesus first appeared to apostles in room / on a mountain.
Luke 24:33,36,37; John 20:19 / Mt 28:16,17

Jesus ascended from Mount Olivet / Bethany.
Acts 1:9,12 / Luke 24:50,51

Paul's attendants heard miraculous voice and stood / didn't hear and were prostrate.
Acts 9:7 / Acts 22:9; Acts 26:14

Betrayal of Jesus

Abraham departed for Canaan / unknown destination.
Gen 12:5 / Heb 11:8

Abraham had two / one sons.
Gal 4:22 / Heb 11:17

Keturah was Abraham's wife / concubine.
Gen 25:1 / 1 Chron 1:32

Abraham had one / six sons at 100, with / without providence.
Gen 21:2; Rom 4:19; Heb 11:12 / Gen 25:1,2

Jacob / Abraham bought a sepulchre from Hamor.
Josh 24:32 / Acts 7:16

God promised Canaan to Abraham and seed forever / Abraham and seed never received promised land.
Gen 13:14,15,17; Gen 17:8 / Acts 7:5; Heb 11:9,13

Goliath / Goliath's brother was slain by Elhanan.
2 Sam 21:19 / 1 Chron 20:5

Ahaziah began reign in 12th / 11th year of Joram.
2 Kings 8:25 / 2 Kings 9:29

Michal had no / five children.
2 Sam 6:23 / 2 Sam 21:8

David was tempted by the Lord / by Satan, to number Israel.
2 Sam 24:1 / 1 Chron 21:1

Fighting men of Israel 800,000 / 1,100,000, Judah 500,000 / 470,000.
2 Sam 24:9 / 1 Chron 21:5

David sinned numbering Israel / never sinned except concerning Uriah.
2 Sam 24:10 / 1 Kings 15:5

Penalty for David's sin was seven / three years famine.
2 Sam 24:13 / 1 Chron 21:11,12

David took 700 / 7000 horsemen.
2 Sam 8:4 / 1 Chron 18:4

David bought threshing floor for 50 silver / 600 gold shekels.
2 Sam 24:24 / 1 Chron 21:25

David's throne to last forever / was cast down.
Ps 89:35-37 / Ps 89:44

Jesus is / is not equal to God.
John 10:30; Phil 2:5 / John 14:28; Mt 24:36

Additional Contradictions

Jesus is / is not all-powerful.
Mt 28:18; John 3:35 / Mark 6:5

Law was / was not ended by Christian dispensation.
Luke 16:16; Eph 2:15; Rom 7:6 / Mt 5:17-19

Jesus' mission was / was not peace.
Luke 2:13,14 / Mt 10:34

Jesus did / did not receive testimony from man.
John 15:27 / John 5:33,34

Jesus' witness of himself is true / not true.
John 8:18,14 / John 5:31

It was lawful / unlawful for the Jews to put Jesus to death.
John 19:7 / John 18:31

Children are / are not punished for parents sins.
Ex 20:5 / Ezek 18:20

Man is / is not justified by faith alone.
Rom 3:20; Gal 2:16; Gal 3:11,12; Rom 4:2 / James 2:21,24; Rom 2:13

It is impossible / possible to fall from grace.
John 10:28; Rom 8:38,39 / Ezek 18:24; Heb 6:4-6; 2 Pet 2:20,21

No man is without sin / Christians are sinless.
Prov 20:9; Eccl 7:20; Rom 3:10 / 1 John 3:9,6,8

Resurrection of the dead / no resurrection of the dead.
Cor 15:52; Rev 20:12,13; Luke 20:37; 1 Cor 15:16 / Job 7:9; Eccl 9:5; Is 26:14

Reward and punishment to be on this world / next world.
Prov 11:31 / Rev 20:12; Mt 16:27; 2 Cor 5:10

Annihilation for all mankind / endless misery for some.
Job 3:11,13-17,19-22; Eccl 9:5,10; Eccl 3:19,20 / Mt 25:46; Rev 20:10,15; Rev 14:11; Dan 12:2

Earth will / will never be destroyed.
2 Pet 3:10; Heb 1:11; Rev 20:11 / Ps 104:5; Eccl 1:4

Evil does not / does happen to the godly.
Prov 12:21; 1 Pet 3:13 / Heb 12:6; Job 2:3,7

Worldly good and prosperity / misery and destruction are the lot of the godly.
Prov 12:21; Ps 37:28,32,33,37; Ps 1:1,3; Gen 39:2; Job 42:12 / Heb 11:37,38; Rev 7:14; 2 Tim 3:12; Luke 21:17

Betrayal of Jesus

Worldly prosperity a reward of righteousness and a blessing / a curse and a bar to future reward.
Mark 10:29,30; Ps 37:25; Ps 112:1,3; Job 22:23,24; Prov 15:6 / Luke 6:20; Mt 6:19,21; Luke 16:22; Mt 19:24; Luke 6:24

Christian yoke is / is not easy.
Mt 11:28-30 / 2 Tim 3:12; Heb 12:6,8

Fruit of the spirit is love and gentleness / vengeance and fury.
Gal 5:22 / Judg 15:14; 1 Sam 18:10,11

Longevity enjoyed by / denied to the wicked.
Job 21:7,8; Ps 17:14; Eccl 8:12; Is 65:20 / Eccl 8:13; Ps 55:23; Prov 10:27; Heb 36:14; Eccl 7:17

Poverty is a blessing / riches a blessing / neither a blessing.
Luke 6:20,24; James 2:5; Prov 10:15; Job 22:23,24 ; 42:12; Prov 30:8,9

Wisdom a source of enjoyment / vexation, grief, sorrow.
Prov 3:13,17 / Eccl 1:17,18

A good name is a blessing / curse.
Eccl 7:1; Prov 22:1 / Luke 6:26

Laughter commended / condemned.
Eccl 3:1,4; Eccl 8:15 / Luke 6:25; Eccl 7:3,4

Rod is remedy for foolishness / there is no remedy.
Prov 22:15 / Prov 27:22

A fool should be / not be answered according to his folly.
Prov 26:5 / Prov 26:4

Prophesy is / not sure.
2 Pet 1:19 / Jer 18:7-10

Man's life was to be 120 / 70 years.
Gen 6:3 / Ps 90:10

Fear of man put upon every beast / but not the lion.
Gen 9:2 / Prov 30:30

Miracles proof / not proof of divine mission.
Mt 11:2-5; John 3:2; Ex 14:31 / Ex 7:10-12; Deut 13:1-3; Luke 11:19

Elijah went up to heaven / only Jesus ascended to heaven.
2 Kings 2:11 / John 3:13

All scripture is inspired / some scripture is not inspired.
2 Tim 3:16 / 1 Cor 7:6,12; 2 Cor 11:17

7

SPECIAL PROBLEMS FOR CATHOLICS

The Catholic Church was conceived in political, not spiritual, expediency and was birthed in chauvinism and oppression. Prior to the formation of a "Catholic" or universal unification, the Christian movement was diverse and a center of lively, vibrant debate.

Prior to this "universal" standardization, there were many diverse sects, from the Gnostics to the Johannine Community to the Pauline conservatives who would eventually form the core of Catholic unification. They had many differing gospels and other scriptural accounts; the New Testament was not standardized into the consistent collection until after unification was completed. At that time, many of the other gospels and texts not accepted into the canon of scripture by the Catholic Church were destroyed. We know many of them only through references about them in other texts that have survived. We have found a few of them, including Gnostic gospels of Mary Magdalene, Peter, Phillip and even Judas Iscariot that were included in the discoveries of ancient texts preserved as the Dead Sea Scrolls.

Origins of Modern Christian Theology

It is ironic that, today, many conservative and Evangelical Protestant sects regard Catholics as not being true Christians.

Primarily, this is the result of Catholics' determination to reconcile (and deny) the contradictions between Jesus' teaching of salvation through universal compassionate love expressed in deeds, and Paul's doctrine of salvation is through faith apart from deeds. The Protestants, basing their views on the teachings of John Calvin that would not be developed until many centuries later, simply throw out the teachings attributed to Jesus, after whom they call themselves, and accept fully the teaching of Paul, who never even met Jesus and got his start as a persecutor of Christians. To whatever extent the Catholics at least try to maintain some inclusion of Jesus' teachings (along with the Mormons, Jehovah's Witnesses and others whose status as legitimate Christians is also challenged by the Evangelicals), then in the contradiction between Jesus and Paul they are at least coming down on the side of their nominal founder whom they regard iconically as the "Son of God" and "Lord and Savior" while rejecting much of what he actually taught. The problem for all of them, however, is that they all deny any such contradiction exists in the first place.

What is further amazing is that many of the sects that deny Catholics their status as legitimate Christians wholly embrace the early creeds (Nicene, Athanasian, Apostolic) which were developed by none other than those very Catholics, after they had come together to form a unified, universal Church.

Special Problems for Catholics

And these same Protestants have adopted almost exactly the same selection of ancient writings that these same Catholics (led initially by Eusebius in the early 4th century) decided of the widely-used early texts were to be considered the canonical Word of God, and they have rejected as scripture the same works that were rejected by these Catholics.

In large part, the rejected texts consisted of the Gnostic Gospels, and the Gospels of Mary Magdalene, Thomas, and even Judas, which presented dissenting views of what would become the male-dominated dogma centered around the letters of Paul and the gospels that could be most easily reconciled with Paul. (As noted in Chapter Four, the letter of James directly contradicts Paul, and there was great discussion over whether or not to include it, but it barely got accepted because the idea of rejecting a letter from the brother of Jesus was too much even for these protectors of male supremacy and the Pauline dogma.)

For a movement so quick to question the right of others to call themselves Christians (because they share the common belief in Jesus as Son of God and Savior), these Protestants have certainly been quick to build the entire core of their theology upon the foundations bequeathed to them by these very "heretics" they disparage.

That said, while it is important to understand the critical role of the Catholic unification in the establishment and proliferation of modern Christianity — and to acknowledge that, however different, Catholics are indeed Christian — there are some specific and problematic points of difference that apply to Catholics separately from other Christians.

It is also extremely important to recognize the difference between engaging in a philosophical discussion about the rational and intellectual merits of the theological claims of

Betrayal of Jesus

Catholicism as a religious tradition, and attacking Catholic people or engaging in anti-Catholic hate speech.

Every organization or institution of human origins, especially if it is has existed over a lengthy period of time, will have been plagued by dark chapters in its history, and faulty leadership of its fallible mortal leaders. Identifying such human failings is not meant to denigrate individual members who are loyal and faithful and sincere in their beliefs, or to ridicule sacred rituals and observances or to undo the many great and noble achievements of the organization. The point is to note that these human foibles demonstrate that the Catholic Church is an institution of human origins and guidance; it is not instituted or ordained by an omniscient, omnipotent or all-worthy deity. It is not God's instrument on earth; it is the fallible mortal effort of fallible mortal humans. The litany of special problems for Catholics could not exist in an institution created and overseen by an all-knowing, all-powerful, all-worthy and all-loving inerrant and infallible deity.

Historical Injustices

The fact of centuries of official historical acts of social and individual injustice is well -known and, with apology, even recognized by the Church. Many consider that these are "old news" and deal with problems that have been corrected. The willingness of the Church to recognize past error and reform is admirable (if not almost always greatly tardy), but this does not justify sweeping old items under the rug.

The Catholic Church claims to be God's Church on Earth. It ascribes infallibility to its leader, the Pope, the "Father" of God's Kingdom on Earth. It is a matter of ecclesiastical integrity that a Church that claims infallibility for its leader and Divine Authority, should have the capacity to maintain a higher standard of integrity than an institution comprised of and operated by admittedly fallible humans. Because of the human element, it might not be realistic to expect absolute perfection, but the awesome scope of violence, corruption, murder and pure evil is astounding.

Because these crimes and sins have been acknowledged by the Church and, for the most part, rectified (with apology) it is not necessary to rehash all the details in depth. But it is important to list them all in a single place, take a close look at them, and ask if it is at all seriously possible to believe that the organization instituted on Earth to reflect God's will for the betterment of his creations, could be allowed to go so far as to commit some of the following atrocities:

Inquisition & Crusades: Massive, widespread genocide against Jews and other non-Christians, and the initiation of unprovoked military invasions of distant, non-threatening nations for purely religious reasons.

Persecution of Jews: In addition to the genocidal Inquisition, there has been long-standing persecution of Jews in pogroms and other harassment for many centuries prior to and following the Inquisition.

Persecution of Science: The Catholic Church opposed most scientific knowledge, long after it was widely known and generally accepted on a consensus basis among experts, including the knowledge that the Earth was round (dating back to calculations by Eratosthenes in 260 BC), to the discovery of planetary motions by Galileo and Newton and the discovery by Copernicus that the Earth moves around the sun, to evolution, and to many other scientific truths. In most cases, the Catholic Church was eventually forced to admit its error and adopt scientific reality, often after hundreds of years of having taken the opposite positions.

Betrayal of Jesus

Witch burning: Joan of Arc, executed for heresy in 1431 at the age of 19, was but one of many who were burned at the stake or waterboarded or hanged because someone suspected an independent young woman or and eccentric older woman or bold, free-thinking woman of any age who was seen as being just a little too odd (or politically dangerous) for their tastes.

Genocide, Enslavement and "Convert-or-die" forced conversions of Aboriginal Peoples: Catholic nations of Spain and Portugal, under agreements adjudicated by Papal decree, conquered by brute force and then killed or enslaved entire populations of aboriginal, indigenous peoples in their defeated colonies, primarily in Latin America and the Philippines and then, even after these populations obtained independence and the official end of slavery, perpetuated their continued economic oppression in two-tiered economies in which the native populations remained impoverished laborers creating wealth to support the opulent lifestyles of the wealthy descendants of the European conquerors.

History of Papal Corruption: In the 14th and 15th centuries, the papacy and hierarchy of cardinals became increasingly corrupt, selling indulgences, dealing in financial bribes, and extensive sexual misbehavior, including multiple mistresses and Popes having sex with children, including in the case of the infamous Borgia popes, their own children (hey, why is a Pope having children anyway?). It was the expansion of this corruption that led to the protests by Martin Luther and others that resulted in both the Protestant Reformation and internal efforts to reform the Church. It can hardly be believed that the level of perversity and widespread, open corruption could possibly have represented God's church on earth.

Special Problems for Catholics

Modern Injustices

World War II Nazis and Pope Pius XII

Pope Pius XII reigned as Pope from 1939, as war was breaking out in Europe, until his death in 1958 at age 82. With the Vatican in a location surrounded by an Italy under Mussolini's Fascist rule and aligned with Hitler in Nazi Germany, a powerful institution such as the Catholic monolith (but with virtually no military resources) had to walk a delicate balance in order to avoid being repressed by forcible, hostile military action.

Certainly it is understandable that the fledgling Papal administration of Pius XII would seek some measure of caution. At the same time, as a much more courageous Pope of the future, Pope John-Paul II (himself as a Pole having witnessed the oppression of World War II dictators), would demonstrate, while Popes may not command military divisions, they command moral authority. All of Mussolini's Italy, and much of the land under German occupation, was religiously Catholic, including some of the world's most devout followers. A word of moral authority on human rights, genocide or human dignity could have created a moral groundswell that could have toppled dictators and prevented the Holocaust.

By ending his predecessor's ban on the virulently anti-Semitic organization Action Française in 1939, in the first month of his administration, Pius XII signaled to many an eagerness to exert hostility toward the Jews.

In June of 1939, still new in office, Pius XII worked with Brazilian emissaries to tighten Brazilian standards for issuing immigration visas, implementing standards that made it increasingly difficult for Jews and other non-Christians to obtain visas, preventing many from escaping the Holocaust.

Betrayal of Jesus

Pius XII disregarded advise of many cardinals and other close advisors as to oppression and persecution of Jews, and refused to follow recommendations that could have reduced such atrocities. He repeatedly refused to publicly denounce the Nazi violence against Jews, despite encouragement from his advisors to do so.

In 1942, during the height of Japanese military aggression, Pius XII established diplomatic relations with the Japanese Empire, allies of the Nazis and Fascists.

There were many opportunities to stand up against violence toward Jews, but the "infallible" Pope seems to have forgotten that Jesus, the purported founder of the seat from which he reigns, was himself a Jew and, if Jesus had been living in the 1940's instead of almost two thousand years earlier, he likely would have died in a gas chamber instead of dangling on a cross.

Protection of Child Abusers

While Popes and others at the top of the Catholic hierarchy have long given lip service to opposing child sexual abuse, my position would be that it is a long-standing official policy of the Catholic Church to endorse and support this reprehensible and disgusting practice, which is otherwise universally and vehemently opposed by all other persons of decency. In fact, I wrestled with whether or not to include this with historical or modern injustices since it has been going on for so long, but since the section on ancient wrongs deals with subjects that no longer apply today, and child abuse by priests is a current issue, I am treating it as a modern issue.

One cannot just dismiss the child sex abuse scandals as aberrant behaviors by a few perverted lone wolves acting in individual betrayal of their faith and vows. All institutions that deal with children, such as public schools, Boy Scouts,

Special Problems for Catholics

Big Brothers and Sisters, summer camps, and churches of other denominations have had to face the rare tragedies of such betrayals, yet they have not been tarnished by the same taint as the Catholic Church.

The reason for the difference is that other institutions do not have official policies to promote and encourage such disgusting practices. In the rare cases where abuse of any kind is even hinted at, other institutions react immediately and with the full force of law enforcement, firing, and openly and aggressively separating themselves from the perpetrators. They do not move the perpetrators to new areas with new victims; they cooperate with law enforcement quickly and aggressively.

In contrast, the Catholic Church has had official policies of covering up the abuse, protecting the abuser instead of the victim, and reassigning the perpetrators to new assignments, where they are exposed (in all meanings of the word) to a fresh supply of new victims. The Council of American Bishops' report by their National Review Board, on February 27, 2004 officially acknowledged with apology their failings and their role in the scandal because of these widespread, official practices. Furthermore, after the American Bishops passed a "zero tolerance" policy to repent and change the course of these immoral policies, the Vatican *rejected* the Americans' action, leaving pedophiliac abuse as still the *official policy of the Catholic Church*. And after Cardinal Bernard Law *(out*law?) of the Boston archdiocese faced possible charges for criminal complicity in abetting known abusers, the same Catholic Church that had abetted the perpetrators also protected him. Pope John Paul II, one of the most beloved of Popes, transferred him to hiding (openly) and protection in Rome.

The Church claims that it was unaware of the magnitude of the abuse, but this is simply dishonest. It is now revealed that in one archdiocese alone, Los Angeles, California, more than 200 priests were involved, and detailed records of the problem were maintained. And it is nothing new. As far back as 1759, 250 years ago, the French philosopher Voltaire wrote to identify and oppose this terrible offense against decency in his masterpiece *Candide*.

When Cardinal Roger Mahony, Archbishop of the Los Angeles Diocese, ceases his years-long obstruction of justice and refusal to cooperate with authorities (which has not occurred as of this writing), and when the Vatican ceases harboring of Cardinal Law, only then will they begin to have a modicum of credibility in their denial of official policies to harbor the criminal child rapists.

Ongoing denial of Equal Rights for Women and those those in the LGBT Community: The ongoing denial of equal rights for women to full participation in Church leadership and government, as well as freedom to control their own reproductive self-determination, is well known, as is their denial of full equality for lesbians, gays, bisexual and transgendered persons. The Church does not deny these official policies of oppression, but openly embraces them as official Church doctrine.

Issues of Doctrine, Ritual and Observance

Idolatry and Graven Images

The Second Commandment (from the Ten Commandments) says: "Thou shalt not make unto thee any graven image, or any likeness of anything..." [Exodus 20:4]

That is pretty explicit. The Moslems, who also claim to be descendants of Abraham through Ishmael, also have a

Special Problems for Catholics

variation of this Commandment in the Koran (Qur'an), in Sûrah 6:103 and 42:11, which for many centuries they interpret so literally as to forbid any images or statues of any kind, including photographs, though recent technological advancement has relaxed this to some extent, though images of God or their prophet Mohammed, especially in ridicule, still evoke tremendous negative reactions.

In clear violation of this, Catholics (as well as some Protestants), maintain elaborate statues of Jesus, Mary and many of the apostles, and often pray to these. What is even more degrading is that many of these depict Jesus at his worst, hanging lifeless upon an implement of capital punishment, and many even wear miniature versions of these ghoulish accolades to the death of their "Lord" around their necks, some with the bloody corpse still dangling on the cross!

While I do understand that this has become commonplace to the point of numbing normal, decent human sensibilities among the faithful, please try to understand how this might look to someone from the outside.

Elaborate, Opulent Lifestyles, Costumes, Rituals

Jesus lived a simple life and honored the poor. He washed the feet of his apostles, and touched and ministered to those considered unclean: the lepers, the prostitutes and the hated enemies from Samaria, the Samaritans.

In stark contrast to all that Jesus lived and died for, the hierarchy of the Catholic church lives and functions in elaborate cathedrals and chapels, with ornate artworks, bedecked in elaborate costumes, performing complex rituals completely unknown to Jesus, with no scriptural basis, and which are not only beyond anything Jesus actually practiced, but out of character with Jesus' entire persona and ministry.

BETRAYAL OF JESUS

Oppression of Women; Male Domination; Celibate Priests

As noted earlier in this chapter, the early efforts to unify the many early sects of Christianity, with their competing doctrines, dogmas and even scriptures, came down to a political difference between those seeking to base their teachings on the words of Jesus, recorded by those who knew him best such as Mary Magdalene, Thomas — even Judas — with their egalitarian perspective of uplifting the poor, meek and disenfranchised (such as women) and the male-dominated followers of the Pauline teachings.

Of course, it is the Pauline authoritarian view that won out and, as a result, despite its complete lack of support in scripture, a tradition began of limiting the role of women. Women would not be allowed key roles in ecclesiastical leadership, and priests would not even be allowed to marry them, much less count them among their ranks.

Celibate priests: Forbidding women in Priesthood may be consistent with the traditions of the sexist culture out of which Judeo-Christian dogma arose, but forbidding priests to marry at a time when the church is desperate for more priests is not only a poor strategy for cultivating dynamic, vibrant leadership, but also a direct contradiction to scripture!

The same church that considers Peter to be the first pope disregards scriptural reference to the fact that the first Holy Father was ... *married!* Matthew 8:14 makes reference to the mother of Peter's wife.

Even Paul warned that forbidding marriage should be seen as a sign of apostasy from his true church [I Timothy 4:3].

The requirement of celibacy deters many vibrant, quality men, and many of those remaining, who are willing to at least live under the pretense of celibacy, are those who do not fit comfortably with the narrow range of traditional family

Special Problems for Catholics

options permitted by those who, admittedly, have the least experience with the subject.

A person who is attracted to those of the same gender is not welcomed into a loving, stable, appropriate family relationship and, shunned, may find refuge in the very clergy that has created a standard impossible for them to live up to. A condition of same-sex attraction, that might have afforded a perfectly normal, stable, family lifestyle if permitted to be enjoyed openly, is perverted by this tragic policy into something hidden, dirty, and which creates guilt and tensions that can build up until what could have been a happy, joyous expression of normal love and commitment, becomes manifest instead into inappropriate attempts at relationships.

Similarly, those who are attracted to children or other objects of affection that, because of the incapacity for valid consent or any semblance of equitable relationship, could *never* be appropriate, may also seek refuge in the dark shadowy corners of an institution where the normal, healthy relationships that should be encouraged are shunned.

Aside from being contrary to scripture, counterproductive toward the goals of expanding a vibrant, dynamic clergy, and putting clergy in a position where they are required to give counsel on areas of life they have no experience with, the policy promotes a tragic perversion of relationships in ways that are wholly unnecessary.

Contributing to Overpopulation and Disease While Ignoring It's Consequences

While hard-working Catholic immigrants from Ireland (including some of my ancestors), Poland, Philippines and Latin America, have contributed to economic and cultural richness of this country working in conjunction with the Protestant, Jewish and other assorted contributors to our multi-cultural admixture. However, I also note that if you look at the modern nations of the world that have grown out of the colonies established by Catholic Spain (Latin America, Philippines) you will find that the hierarchical power structures, forbidding of population control, and concentration of wealth in the hands of the Spanish conquerors and their descendants and the virtual enslavement of the indigenous populations, has resulted in a legacy of these nations being among the most impoverished of any in the world, especially in comparison with the former colonies of Protestant English, Dutch or German colonizers.

Opposition to abortion, but especially birth control (Latin America, Philippines and other predominantly Catholic countries are among poorest and most backward in world) is an example of how Catholicism has not blessed the existences of the "least of these," but rather has magnified the suffering of god's beloved poor.

Forbidding even the use of condoms to prevent AIDS while also doing very little to constructively address the issue further exemplifies the contempt for the real needs of the poorest of the poor, while doing too little too late to react to the symptoms of poverty and disease that are the direct results of Catholic institutional policies.

Looking Ahead

It is possible that the elevation of Cardinal Archbishop Jorge Mario Bergoglio of Argentina to become Pope Francis, the first ever Jesuit to attain the papacy, might offer reason for optimism for future reforms, especially in the areas of social and economic issues and a rejection of some of the past opulence and excesses towards a simpler, more humble papacy.

However, Francis' past writings and statements do not offer as much hope in matters of equal rights for women or gays/lesbians, or for reforms such as softening the rigid adherence to a celibate clergy, or easing the harsh demands for increased procreation and the poverty it breeds. But when one considers the realistic range of choices for a successor to Pope Benedict, who was one of the most corrupt pontiffs in centuries and the chief architect of the official policy of protecting and harboring child rapists, and that so many of the voting cardinals had been appointed by him, there were certainly none that were *less* conservative on social issues, and none that were more liberal on issues of social and economic justice. The elevation of Pope Francis certainly does not dissolve all the issues of the Catholic church, but surely it is a refreshing breath of fresh air and may represent a small step towards much-needed reform.

Conclusions

To restate, it is important to understand that these criticisms are offered by way of rational discussion as to the theological claims of the Catholic Church to be God's ordained and established institution on Earth.

This litany of failings is not meant to disparage sincere, faithful believers, or to undermine the many programs by which the Church today does do much good in the world. It is also not intended to lose sight of the fact that any large institution with thousands of years of history will have had its dark chapters and shady characters, but that is the point: the Church is a *human* institution — the best effort of sincere but fallible mortals, and *not* something instituted by an all-knowing, all-powerful, all-loving inerrant or infallible deity.

8

Special Problems for Mormons

As Christians who put a messianic belief in Jesus Christ as the central doctrine of their faith, adherents to the Church of Jesus Christ of Latter-day Saints, more commonly known as "Mormons" from their belief in the *Book of Mormon* as the scriptural Word of God in addition to the Bible, share many of the same problems of theology as other Christians.

While most of the points made earlier are targeted to more traditional mainstream and evangelical Christians, and some details may not apply to specific variations in Mormon beliefs, most of the concepts do apply to some extent to Mormon theology.

For example, while Mormons do allow some wiggle room on accepting inerrancy or infallibility of the Bible "as far as it is translated correctly" and thus can get around some details in contradictions, major Biblical contradictions that address key doctrinal conflicts are still problematic, as are contradictions between the Bible and other Mormon scriptures. Because the Book of Mormon claims to be "revealed" by God directly to his chosen prophet for modern times, a humble farm boy named Joseph Smith, Jr., Mormons can claim this book to be without "translation errors." However, the claims for how this book came to be revealed, and the claim that it has no internal contradictions or factual errors that could be attributed to "translation errors," do not stand up to careful scrutiny, as we shall see.

Further, issues of Christian theology such as the problem of Paul's contradiction with Jesus and James (Mormons differ from evangelical Protestants by coming down in favor of Jesus/James rather than Paul, ironically causing those who follow Paul instead of Jesus to accuse the Mormons of not being legitimate Christians) are still problematic because of the contradiction itself. Also, while some specific details about a belief in Jesus' atoning blood sacrifice for sin differ from traditional and evangelical Protestants, Mormons do believe in the concept of sin transference and that Jesus took upon himself the sins of others, thus "paying the price" for our sins, and so most of the concerns regarding Paul's doctrine of blood atonement, while differing in some details, still apply generally to Mormons as well.

Theological Integrity

The wide variety of religious beliefs, not only among Christians but also around the world, for the most part reflects humans' varying attempts to explain a complicated universe. Religious myths are the best efforts by fallible mortals to explain a universe beyond their comprehension. That they differ merely reflects the different thought processes of differing individuals and cultures. In many cases, the written accounts

Special Problems for Mormons

of myths are committed to written form many centuries after the alleged events are written, and they are not scribed into a sacred canon with the intent to deceive but to reflect the best understanding of dramatic tales that have been embellished and enhanced through years of retelling in a time when imperfect memories were not aided by cameras, videotape or formalized documentation.

Once certain assumptions are made, such as an acceptance that Jesus is a Messianic atoning Savior, differing sects can extrapolate varying tangential or derivative secondary beliefs in different ways. Occasionally, though, someone comes along and simply makes up grandiose claims that are outright fraudulent. Hucksters come along selling miracle cures, and faith healers claim to perform miraculous healings while getting rich in the process. While most Christian sects evolved through honest questioning and sincere efforts at seeking the truth, Mormonism originates entirely as a hoax, arising out of a dramatic attempt at outright and deliberate fraud: claims of divine and miraculous interventions that are completely fabricated, with new revelations along with claims of ancient texts discovered and translated through divine assistance.

It is also important to take a balanced view. Especially in the last 60 years, under the leadership of such forward-looking Presidents as David O. McKay and Spencer W. Kimball, the Mormon church has been able to shed many of the more extreme vestiges of its strange history and origins, and fit more gracefully into mainstream society. The current church president, Thomas S. Monson and his predecessor, Gordon B. Hinckley, have continued this trend. Additional Mormon emphasis on family, education, industriousness, actual compliance with behavioral standards rather than mere lip service, and contributing to their communities make them real assets to their neighborhoods and strong, valued, loyal friends. Having enjoyed the privilege of close friendship with several Mormons, I sincerely respect their character, personal integrity and sincerity, but at the same time recognize that they are the innocent, well-intentioned victims of a very elaborate hoax that was concocted long before any modern Mormons, members or leaders, had been born.

Let us examine some of the unique issues that apply only to Mormons, largely because of their belief that their church was founded by divine revelation to Joseph Smith based on personal visits by God the Father, Jesus Christ the Son and numerous other angelic and divine visitors. Some of these problems arise out of the story of how these events unfolded, and some directly to flaws in Mormon scriptures themselves.

The First Vision and Joseph Smith's Revelations

The "First Vision" is a basic story taught to every Mormon child and all new converts. It is a simple story that is easy to learn and remember. Few have difficulty recalling it or keeping it straight, for years at a time, even after just hearing it a few times.

The official version of this story is recounted in the Mormon scriptures known as the Pearl of Great Price, in the Book of Joseph Smith II. The account was written by Smith in 1842, just two years before he was murdered while in jail. The story is that in the spring of 1820, when he was 14 years old, there was a great religious revival in upstate New York where he lived, with competing denominations seeking to attract members. Various members of the Smith family were pulled in different directions, and Joseph Smith, torn by competing claims, and following the advice of James 1:5 to seek wisdom by asking it directly from God in prayer, went into the woods to pray.

In response to this simple prayer by a humble fourteen year old, a dramatic event of literally earth-shaking proportions occurred: God the Father personally appeared to young Joseph, along with Jesus Christ. Literally. In the flesh (confirming the corporeal rather than spiritual nature of deity). Joseph, face to face with God the Father and his Son Jesus Christ, asked them which church he should join and they said none were true and that he had been selected to "restore" the true Church of Jesus Christ that had been lost from the earth through a widespread apostasy.

It's a pretty simple story — easy enough to remember. Millions of Mormons learn this as one of their earliest introductions to the faith, either from their parents if born into the Church or as new converts, and even non-Mormons have no difficulty keeping the basic story straight. It is memorable, dramatic, powerful, and easy to remember.

This initial visit was augmented by subsequent visitations from an angel named Moroni that led to the bringing forth of the *Book of Mormon,* and yet further heavenly visitors would come to "restore" powers of various levels of "priesthood" as well as various rites, rituals and ordinances.

The problem is that this "official" 1842 account, enshrined as official Mormon scripture, doesn't match the personal history and accounts of Joseph Smith himself or the recollections of his own family.

Especially problematic for Mormons has been the 1853 biography of Joseph Smith by his own mother, Lucy Mack Smith. Note that young fourteen-year-old Joselph was still living at home with Lucy through most of the dramatic events he described in his "First Vision," which he claims caused such a stir, but she cannot keep his simple story at all straight, remembering key details quite differently. The

Betrayal of Jesus

Mormon Church eventually solved this dilemma by simply making up their own alternative edition, but can't escape the thorny problem that many copies of the original still exist.

According to award-winning UCLA historian Fawn M. Brodie[*], Joseph Smith's first published autobiographical sketch, written in 1834 along with the first published history of the church the same year, did not even mention the incident. This would have been four years after the 1830 official founding of his new Church of the Latter-Day Saints (later re-named Church of Jesus Christ of Latter-Day Saints) and fourteen years after the supposed earth-shaking event. Unpublished accounts by others show a profound evolution of this event, from having the Lord opening the heavens (1931) to seeing God alone to seeing God and Jesus with many angels, to changes in the date it occurred. Joseph's brother, William, and his mother, Lucy, reported that he never said anything about it at the time, and years later they had great difficulty keeping this simple story straight, though they lived with him at the time it supposedly occurred, while millions of modern Mormons have no such difficulty. In contrast, Joseph claimed in the official 1842 account that he told numerous people, and that his widespread dissemination of his account caused a great stir, such that "men of high standing" would take great notice of "an obscure boy, only between fourteen and fifteen years of age ... a boy of no consequence in the

---

[*] Fawn M. Brodie, *No Man Knows My History,* (New York: Alfred A Knopf, 1945) p. 21-25. Ms. Brodie was a Pulitzer Prize winning professor of History at University of California, Los Angeles (UCLA) and a Los Angeles Times Woman of the Year. She was born and raised in the Mormon religion and her uncle, David O. McKay was the ninth President (prophet, seer and revelator) of the Church of Jesus Christ of Latter-Day Saints (Mormon). She also wrote best-selling historical biographies of Thomas Jefferson and Richard Nixon. All of her works represent first-class scholarly research supported by extensive documentation.

Special Problems for Mormons

world" (Pearl of Great Price; Joseph Smith 2:21-23). However, extensive review of local publications of that time by historian Brodie indicated no such furor, though they did report on the local revival activity.

In short, Joseph Smith claimed to have a dramatic, earth-shaking event in the spring of 1820, when he was 14 years old, that stirred up the community. Yet there are no contemporary accounts of any such reports, his own family remembers hearing nothing about it until years later, and the first published accounts of his own autobiography and early church histories fail to mention it altogether. Yet once the story was concocted, some time in the late 1830's, after evolving through various permutations until settling into the standardized form now canonized in Mormon scripture, it became the centerpiece of Mormon lore, and an account that is now both central and unforgettable to modern Mormons and no one has a hard time keeping it straight.

Joseph Smith and "Modern Scripture"

The Book of Mormon

We have noted that the pivotal historical account of Mormon tradition, Joseph Smith's "First Vision," seems to be something that was invented many years after the fact. In contrast, the real beginnings of the Mormon movement originate with the coming forth of the Book of Mormon.

Initially, this did not begin as a religious venture. While Joseph Smith's initial introduction of what would become the Book of Mormon did include some of the common supernatural elements of the day, such as encounters with angels or spirits and the discovery of artifacts with magic powers to make up for a lack of credentials or qualifications, Smith initially just wanted to develop and market a theory of where the ancient American Indian peoples had come from, concocting a hybridized compilation of several common theories floating around at the time. Some time around 1827, Smith had apparently found some Indian artifacts including a breast plate and some jeweled stones similar to others that had been found in the area and that can still be found in museums. He called the stones the Urim and Thummim after a Biblical reference, and claimed that looking through them gave him great powers of discernment. He also claimed that an angel had entrusted him with the care of some golden plates, upon which were written the accounts of the ancient peoples of the land. Unlike his descriptions of the First Vision, this account was his first such account and one that remained remarkably consistent and which his family had no difficulty remembering. Unlike the breastplate and "Urim and Thummim," no one was allowed to see the mysterious golden plates, which he always kept hidden.

Using the "Urim and Thummim" seer stones (which some mockingly derided as "magic glasses"), and with the financial aid and clerical assistance of a local farmer named Martin Harris, Joseph Smith "translated" 116 pages of the ancient Indians' history. Aside from the initial assistance of the angel, there were no revelations and no visions or other reports of divine intervention, and the work was not religious in nature; it contained a secular record of the ancient peoples.

In his enthusiastic support, but contrary to Smith's instructions, Martin Harris took the 116 pages to see if he could obtain independent scholarly corroboration and his skeptical wife, fearing that Smith was trying to milk her husband for financial support of his hoax, destroyed them.

When Smith learned what had happened, he was distraught. Harris' wife taunted him that he could just re-trans-

Special Problems for Mormons

late the missing pages, but Smith knew that nothing had actually been "translated" and that he could never duplicate the content close enough that Martin Harris or anyone else who had seen it wouldn't be able to tell the difference.

After several agonizing months, Smith found a solution — one that would transform the direction of his project and change forever the course of American religious history: the work would become religious in nature. Smith had the first of what would become many direct revelations from God and became a prophet. This first revelation, now preserved as Section 3 of the Doctrine and Covenants and still shown as the (chronologically) first revelation of this period, chastised Smith and Harris for betraying their trust over precious artifacts and told them that, as their punishment, they would lose the right to enjoy the fruits of the work that had been translated. But in addition to the secular record that had been lost, the revelation revealed a smaller companion record of God's religious dealings with the same people over the same period of time, and stated that they would be allowed to have this record. So Smith could start anew, still come up with his new volume without having it compared to the one he could never possibly duplicate, and the world would gain a new religious standard, the Book of Mormon, and the establishment of a new religious sect, the Church of the Latter-Day Saints (soon renamed the Church of Jesus Christ of Latter-Day Saints), popularly known as "Mormons" after Smith's invented volume of scripture with the same name.

Errors in God's Newest Word, except for Isaiah

The Book of Mormon as first published contained numerous errors of grammar, punctuation and general literary construction, owing to the limited education of Smith, Harris and his other assistants, most notably Oliver Cowdery who had taken over most of the transcription duties from Martin Harris during the dictation by Smith of his "translation."

On one hand, Mormons claim this to be directly revealed by God (through the Urim and Thummim), making it the "most perfect of all scripture," as Brigham Young later described it. On the other hand, the nascent Church needed to polish its credibility, and so has issued several revisions to clean up word choice, punctuation, grammar and syntax. They justify this by saying that God gave Smith general inspiration, but Smith selected the actual words, which reflected his limited education. But this does not explain the extensive direct copying of the words of Isaiah through massive portions of 2 Nephi (most notably 2 Nephi 12 through 2 Nephi 24, which correspond directly to Isaiah 2 through Isaiah 14, respectively — just one chapter after another, in order, directly copied from Isaiah into 2 Nephi). The words of 2 Nephi that correspond to Isaiah match exactly the words of Isaiah. So when copying existing scripture, God seems to have given the education-challenged Smith the exact words, but then otherwise just gave him general impressions and he chose his own words. Not only do the Isaiah copies use the exact words of Isaiah, but they select the exact words from the King James Version of the Bible, which was no longer the colloquial dialect of this early 19th Century New England village, 200 years after translation by the Royal Court in London, nor is it the best or most accurate translation when considered in light of modern knowledge of linguistics and etymological context. But it does match the only version of the Bible that would have been available in the Smith household in the late 1820's, and is just amazing that God gave exact words for that portion of the translation (or other copied sections) but not for any other. So, which is it? You can accept either that God gave the exact words (as in the passages of copied scriptures) or that he gave general inspiration and Smith picked his own vocabulary, grammar and syntax. But you can't have it both ways.

Wtinesses to the Grand Production

To support his wild claims, Joseph Smith knew he had to get some dramatic evidence. To do this, he enlisted the support of "witnesses" who would testify that they had seen evidence of his miraculous claims.

To this day, at the front of every Book of Mormon, are two sets of Testimonials:

The first is by three selected witnesses — Oliver Cowdery, David Whitmer and Martin Harris — who testified that they saw the golden plates, that they personally beheld an angel of God who came down from heaven before their very eyes and confirmed the veracity of Smith's claims and the validity of his translation, and that they also heard the voice of God booming from the heavens with the same confirmation. Three witnesses! Pretty strong stuff.

The second was a group of eight witnesses — four more from the Whitmer family, a guy named Hiram Page, along with Joseph's father and two of his brothers. They testified that they saw and held the golden plates from which Smith had allegedly translated the Book of Mormon.

All together, that makes a total of 11 witnesses who at least saw the golden plates, with three of them also witnessing an angel and hearing the voice of God.

What is even more amazing is that, in a Church that today prides itself on one of the highest rates of retention of new converts, who have not personally witnessed anything so dramatic as what these 11 testified to, *all three* of the first set of witnesses eventually left the Mormon Church, even after

Betrayal of Jesus

seeing what they claimed to have seen. While the ever-loyal Martin Harris did come crawling back in his old age to a church that greeted him as a repentant hero, the fact remains that of the first three witnesses, *all of them* at some point took the extreme and dramatic step of leaving the church.

And the second group of eight? *All of them* who did not have the last name of Smith also strayed from the church.

Out of these 11 vaunted witnesses, 8 of them, and 100% of those not having the last name of Smith, left the church. What is truly amazing is that the modern Mormon Church has the chutzpah to still boldly print these "testimonies" in the front of every Book of Mormon it gives away.

The Pearl of Great Price

The historical and problems in bringing forth the Book of Mormon pale in comparison to problems with Joseph Smith's later "translation" of Egyptian papyri that became the Pearl of Great Price (PGP).

The Book of Mormon was entirely an outright fraud. Smith just made it up. When hard pressed to show some tangible evidence of the "Gold Bible," Smith was never able to produce anything of substance, but he did later draw up some samples of the writing, which he called "Reformed Egyptian" (no such language or alphabet actually exists).

But, what a difference with the PGP! Joseph Smith had promoted himself as having the ability to translate ancient writings, and the owner of some real Egyptian mummies with accompanying papyri texts in written Egyptian, having heard of Smith's purported abilities as a "translator," sought him out to see if he would be able to translate the papyri texts. For once Smith had something real and tangible in his hot little hands, of verified antiquity, that he could actually (and in

Special Problems for Mormons

proud dramatic style) show people! And, *of course* he could translate it!

And of course, wouldn't you just know it, of all the old Egyptian manuscripts that just happened to find their way to America and then to Smith, these just happened to contain the long lost books of "Abraham" and "Moses." So Smith translated these ancient books and made a new scripture, the Pearl of Great Price.

Unlike his purely imaginative earlier works, he had some real ancient texts he had "worked" from. So, in his excitement and enthusiasm, he even included facsimile pages from these and actually had them published in the PGP, where they still can still be seen, even in current editions. Since Ancient Egyptian was an indecipherable language, Smith must have thought he was safe.

Not only are three actual facsimiles printed in the PGP, but Smith was bold enough to print the purported "translations" of the specific cuts, with specific items numbered in the illustration and the corresponding "translation" for each numbered item accompanying the page with the "facsimile." On page 28 is "Facsimile #1" and, right below it, is the translation. To avoid any confusion as to whether this is just an example of the texts used, the caption to the accompanying "translation" used to be the caption: "Explanation of the Above Cut," followed by said 'translation" of the specifically numbered items. In like fashion, "Facsimile #2" appears on page 34 with the accompanying "translation" appearing on the facing page (p. 35) which used to include a reference to the foregoing page, and "Facsimile #3" appears on page 42 with the translation (as in #1) appearing below it and used to include a reference to the "above cut." While the purported translations are still included in the texts as currently published, the captions stating that the translations match the

121

specific texts were deleted in publications after the 1980's, following widespread dissemination of linguistic challenges showing that the actual Egyptian texts bore not the slightest resemblance to what Smith had claimed they said. One of the most comprehensive compilations of the linguistic evidence against the Pearl of Great Price was developed by Jerald and Sandra Tanner.*

Unbeknownst to Smith, however, a few years earlier Jean-Francois Champollion had broken the code to the Rosetta Stone and, from that foundation came the deciphering of the Egyptian language. Today, Ancient Egyptian texts can easily be read by trained scholars.

Tragically for Smith and the Mormons, modern scholars of Egyptian have had numerous opportunities to review these facsimiles from Smith's original Egyptian mummy-papers (as he so proudly printed in the his own PGP). The good news (for Mormons) is that they were real, honest-to-goodness Ancient Egyptian texts. The bad news (for Mormons) is that they are routine burial documents with nothing particularly memorable to the modern world, and nothing remotely similar to Smith's claims that they are the writings of Abraham and Moses.

A few quotes:

Dr. A.H. Sayce, Oxford University: "Joseph Smith's impudent fraud."

Mr. W.M. Flinders Petrie, London University: "Too absurd to be noticed. It may be safely said that there is not one single word that is true in these explanations."

---

* Jerald and Sandra Tanner, Mormonism: Shadow or Reality, (Salt Lake City: Modern Microfilm Company, 1972) pp. 294-369. This work is also an excellent source of information on the history of the Book of Mormon and the historical changes in Smith's accounts of his visitations by divine beings.

Special Problems for Mormons

Dr. James H. Breasted, University of Chicago: "[Joseph Smith is] absolutely ignorant of the simplest facts of Egyptian writing and civilization."

Dr. Arthur C. Mace, assistant curator, Metropolitan Museum of Art, N.Y., Dept of Egyptian Art, calls the Book of Abraham "pure fabrication."

Professor S.A.B. Mercer, Ph.D., Custodian Hibbard Collection, calls it "pure imagination."

Numerous equally embarrassing studies go into great depth of analysis to explain exactly what the papyri actually say, and to demonstrate in pathetic detail the embarrassing fraud of the Pearl of Great Price.

Contradictions and Errors in LDS Scriptures

Since the entirety of Mormon scriptures is only a fraction of the size of the Bible, it should be expected that there would be proportionately fewer internal contradictions. Add to that the fact that these scriptures were all written by a single creator (from a single perspective) over a relatively short period of time (barely 15 years) compared with the Bible being written by more than 40 writers over several thousand years, and the expected number of contradictions should be further reduced. The fact that *any* such errors at all exist in a work purportedly revealed directly by God is problematic for Mormons. Here are a few examples:

1 Nephi 3:7 asserts that God will never give a commandment that is impossible to obey; however 2 Nephi 2:16-23 says that God gave Adam and Eve conflicting commandments that they had to choose between in order to force them to introduce sin into the world. (And the idea that *God* should need to force them to introudce sin into the world is, itself, morally problematic.)

123

Betrayal of Jesus

Jacob 1:15 says that the polygamous multiple marriages of David and Solomon were "wicked" and Jacob 2:24 says they were "abominable" but Doctrine and Covenants 132:38-39 says those many wives and concubines were given by God and "in nothing did they [David and Solomon] sin." Mormons usually respond to this blatant and direct contradiction by citing that the specific laws relating to marriage may be applied differently in differing eras and conditions. But while one might very well express concern about varying moral laws so drastically, this contradiction is not about that. It is about the specific factual assertions regarding David and Solomon. Were their numerous wives and concubines indicative of their sinful wickedness (as stated in the Book of Mormon) or sinless gifts of God (as stated in the Doctrine and Covenants)?

The text of the Book of Mormon is replete with scores of references throughout its pages to horses and chariots, which did not exist in the New World prior to Columbus.

The Book of Mormon describes great civilizations of ancient America, and certainly there were, indeed, great civilizations by the Incas, Mayas, Aztecs, Toltecs and others, yet while the ancient Biblical sites can be extensively corroborated by archaeological evidence, there is no analogous corroboration of ancient Book of Mormon sites with any of the extensive available data we have regarding ancient sites in the Americas, and none of the place names or descriptions in the Book of Mormon can be matched with any of the many actual archaeological sites of these civilizations. None of the ancient writings, artifacts or reports of oral traditions of legends matches anything in the Book of Mormon.

The Bible may have its share of contradictions, factual errors and failed prophecies, owing to its authorship by fallible mortals, but at least it is of legitimately authentic antiquity. The Mormon scriptures are simply a fraudulent hoax, concocted by a single perpetrator: Joseph Smith, Jr.

Other Issues

Temple Rituals and Masonry

When Joseph Smith first decided to reestablish the ancient Hebrew traditions of Temples, he founded the first of these in Kirtland, Ohio. It is still considered the first Mormon Temple, yet it operated in ways unrecognizable to modern Mormons. Unlike today's Mormon Temples, it was not closed to all but the most faithful of church members, who must literally become card-carrying holders of permits known as "Recommends" following in-depth personal interviews from both local and regional church officials to confirm that they conform in belief and practice to strict Mormon standards.

The original Kirtland Temple, dedicated (formally opened) in 1836, was a place of supernatural visits from divine visitors bringing the "restoration" of Christ's ancient church, special revelation, and important Church-wide gatherings. It was not closed to the general public. It did introduce new rituals including symbolic anointings and ritual washings, but did not include the practice of today's secret (Mormons would say "sacred") rituals, nor did it conduct rituals for dead people as in modern Temples.

After the Mormons were driven out of Ohio, they resettled first in Missouri (which Joseph Smith declared to be the original antediluvian site of the actual Garden of Eden), and after also being driven out of Missouri by angry neighbors, they drained a swamp along the Illinois shore of Mississippi River and built, from scratch, their own city of Nauvoo, Illinois. There, just a few years after the creation of the Kirtland Temple, while awaiting completion of a new Temple in Nauvoo (which would not be completed until after Joseph Smith's assassination) they initiated Temple Rituals unlike anything ever seen in Kirtland, using temporary facilities. Upon completion of permanent Temples, such rituals would be restricted to worthy members in good standing (as certified by their "Recommends") within the hallowed walls of the Temples. These included many of the rituals for both living and dead that remain highly secretive tfor Church members today, often generating much curiosity among outsiders.

What caused the great transformation in ritual practices within a period of less than five years? Mormons, of course, declare that God had given divine instruction through revelation to Joseph Smith. There was, however, one significant intervening event.

Joseph Smith had grown up in New York hearing tales of secret Masonic rituals that supposedly dated back to the original Temple of Solomon. In the Book of Mormon, written while still young, Smith had repeated references to evil "secret societies" and conspiratorial combinations, which were widely interpreted as being anti-Masonic. Perhaps this negative view was the result of envious resentment in knowing that, with his lowly station in life, he would never qualify for admission. By the early 1840's, however, Smith had become a highly influential public person, and was solicited by Masons to become a member. On March 15, 1842, a Masonic Lodge was installed in Nauvoo and Joseph Smith became a Mason. Becoming familiar with the secret rituals, he then adapted them into secret Mormon rituals. Mormons acknowledge the similarity of some aspects of their rites to those of the Masons, but dismiss criticisms of imitation. They claim that any similarities are because both trace their origins to a common source: the ancient Temple of Solomon. They claim that, over the centuries, the Masonic versions became corrupted, thus explaining whatever differences exist, but that both originate from the same source. This claim, of course, would have held far greater plausibility if God had chosen to reveal these ancient secrets directly to Smith *before* he just happened to hear them from the Masons. Many historians surmise that the real reason for Smith's assassination barely two years later was to fulfill the Masons' blood oaths that were to be enforced against anyone betraying their secrets.

Communal Socialism

Along the same lines as the expropriation of the Masonic Temple rites and converting them into a tool of cult membership control, the Mormons also utilized another tool for control of members common to cults.

As with David Koresh of the Branch Davidian cult and Jim Jones of the Jonestown People's Temple cult, and other cults before and since, Smith cited these early First Century Christian socialist communal experiments (See subheading, "Would Jesus Be Liberal or Conservative?" at the end of Chapter 9) as a ploy to get their followers to give up their assets under what he called the "United Order" under a "Law of Consecration" thus increasing their dependence on the cult leader. The cults of Koresh and Jones went down in flames and Kool Aid (actually, FlaVor Aid®) respectively, while the Mormons retreated from their socialist experiments (as they also did with polygamy and mandatory racial discrimination when they became politically incorrect), and tried to fit into the moderate mainstream by repudiating their socialism and becoming staunch economic conservatives. It is reminiscent of the irony of Mitt Romney being the only Republican candidate in the 2008 primary election to have had only one wife, prior to Mike Huckabee's enterance into the race, while coming from a great-grandfather who had managed five of them - at the same time.

"Word of Wisdom"

The so-called "Word of Wisdom" is the "revelation" given to Joseph Smith as section 89 of the Doctrine and Covenants, best known for being interpreted as prohibiting the use of tobacco, alcohol, coffee and tea. The section does mention "wine and strong drinks" though makes no specific mention of beer or spirits. It does specifically prohibit tobacco, but there is no mention of tea or coffee, only "hot drinks" though later Church officials have interpreted this as meaning specifically tea or coffee at any temperature; some individual Mormons also interpret this to prohibit other forms of caffeine, such as in soft drinks, but this is an individual, not official, interpretation.

Section 89 does allow the use of pure grape wine in sacramental observations, however subsequently the sacramental wine was replaced by water, thus symbolically reversing Jesus' first miracle, as reported in John 2:1-11, in which he turned water into wine. Some believe that the fact that Jesus chose the creation of wine out of water to be the first demonstration of his miraculous power has special significance, especially since he commanded its ceremonial consumption as part of his last supper with these disciples, as a means of remembering him in the future (as reported in Matt 26:26-29; Mark 14:22-25; Luke 22:14-20) thus bookending the starting and ending of his ministry with celebrations of wine.

Some Mormons have tried to explain to me that they believe Jesus was merely consuming grape juice. But the Bible repeatedly uses the word "wine," not grape juice, and the consumption of grape juice would have been extremely rare and unusual (and certainly not at a wedding celebration

Special Problems for Mormons

such as at Cana) in the time before the invention of refrigeration or pasteurization, which was not applied to grapes until 1869, when a process was developed by American physician and dentist Thomas Bramwell Welch, founder of Welch's Grape Juice.

Further, Jesus made it clear in Luke 7:33-34 and Matt 11:18-19 that he enjoyed the consumption of wine, noting that others even call him a "winebibber" [according to King James Version] or "drunkard" in more modern translations. The term "drunkard" is not applied to those who drink mere grape juice (especially before it was even viable).

Clearly, the "revelation" claimed by Joseph Smith relegates Jesus to the status of a sinner. Of course, other Christian denominations such as the Seventh-Day Adventists, who also forbid wine, as well as other organizations such as the Women's Christian Temperance Union (WCTU) also have the same problem in condemning the consumption of wine.

Other health standards, such as the commandment to avoid eating meat except in winter or times of famine, hunger or for special celebrations of thanksgiving, are often ignored by modern Mormons, even though modern health sciences concur with warnings about overconsumption of saturated fats that are troublingly abundant in such foods.

And in verse 89:17 Smith "reveals" that wheat is good for humans while oats are for horses and barley for fowl and swine, whereas today modern health sciences teach us that oats and barley are among the most healthful for humans. Much other modern health knowledge, known today but not in Smith's time, is omitted, though one would think that an omniscient deity offering such revelations might have been able to drop in a few hints about health knowledge beyond what was known in Smith's time, such as simple information about aerobic and anaerobic exercises, herbal sources of antioxidants and the value of limited wine consumption.

Racial Apartheid

While official Mormon scriptures (Bible, Book of Mormon, Doctrine and Covenants and Pearl of Great Price) are silent about specific teachings on the subject of race, there were long held to be private, confidential revelations not recorded in "scripture" that specified that the "mark of Cain" from the book of Genesis was a curse of dark skin, and that Africans (and their American descendants through slavery) are the descendants of Cain, surviving the Great Flood through Noah's son Ham who had married Egyptus.

This teaching, not sanctioned in official scripture, was that, in addition to the curse of dark skin, the curse also prohibited any descendant of Cain from being ordained into the Mormon priesthood. This priesthood is not like the priesthoods of other Christian denominations where few are called to a special leadership role, but a lay priesthood in which virtually all adult males participate. Thus, being excluded from the priesthood meant that African Americans were excluded from most aspects of worship, including participation in Temple ceremonies that are required for acceptance into the highest level of the "celestial kingdom" in the next life.

Ironically, when first instituted during the 1830's, the policy was considered one of the most progressive anywhere in the Christian world. At a time when slavery was still practiced, Mormons openly opposed slavery even while in slave states such as Missouri (which was one of a number of reasons for their persecutions there), and at least allowed African Americans membership in the same congregations with whites, except for being denied priesthood roles.

But as the American perspective evolved, first to abolish slavery, then gradually accept all humans to levels of full equality without regard to race, the Mormons did not change with them, and when removal of the last barriers to full and equal civil rights became a major issue during the 1950's and 1960's, the Mormons remained locked in their traditions and became increasingly ostracized for their position. Although not recorded in official scritpure, the practice was believed to come from a secret, unwritten revelation, and thus could not be changed by mere mortals, but only by (literally) an act of God. Many Mormons, weary of being ostracized as pariahs, and many with sincere reservations about the morality of the policy, hoped for such an act of divine revelation, which finally came to church prophet and President Spencer W. Kimball in May of 1978.

Polygamy

As with racial apartheid, the church teaching on polygamy was extremely troubling to many Mormons (as well as a deterrent to potential converts who were repulsed by it). It originated in a "revelation" to Joseph Smith officially on July 12, 1843 (less than a year before his murder) as section 132 of the Doctrine and Covenants. Prior to that there had long been rumors of Smith's many infidelities and sexual adventures, and it seems that with this "revelation" he sought to legitimize his exploits.

Initially, the revelation was circulated only in limited, exclusive circles to those "called" to the practice. At the time the revelation was made public after Smith's death, some Mormons felt that Joseph Smith had become corrupted and a "fallen prophet" and split off from the main branch of the church, and rejected D&C 132. Emma Smith, Joseph's first wife, was never happy about this "revelation" (which conveniently includes a specific "commandment" directed to her to accept Joseph's additional "wives") and, following the struggle for succession to Smith's leadership after his death, Emma split off from the main church and set her son as the prophet of a splinter branch of the faith, called the "Reorganized Church of Jesus Christ of Latter-day Saints." The RLDS has never accepted D&C 132 or the practice of polygamy.

In fairness to the theological integrity of Joseph Smith, as despised as the practice of polygamy had become in the America of European immigrants, it did have strong Biblical support from the Old Testament, as noted in Chapter 9.

After moving to Utah and allowing polygamy to become practiced openly, it became engrained in the culture of Mormon society. And just as splinter groups broke off from the body of the church when polygamy was introduced, so also when it was rescinded by another politically convenient "revelation" to church prophet and President Wilford Woodruff in 1890, splinter groups of those unwilling to give up polygamy also broke off from the main body of the church, calling themselves "Fundamentalist" Mormons (most prominent being the Fundamentalist Church of Jesus Christ of Latter-day Saints or FLDS), and many of their descendants continue to practice polygamy today, in clandestine secrecy, in enclaves primarily centered around southern Utah and northern Arizona, and in isolation through Utah, though the practice today is prohibited by law in Utah and federal U.S. laws, and the modern Mormon church vigorously enforces their prohibition of plural marriage.

Changing Doctrines in response to Social Pressure

As Mormons have done in both of these instances — racial apartheid and polygamy — where they changed long-held religious beliefs, it could be argued that changing conditions might sometimes require changes in the specific practices of religious rituals and observances.

However, in the case of both racial apartheid and polygamy, we are not talking about minor details of social custom or trivialities of conformance with ritualistic observations. We are talking about fundamental moral issues that affect the deepest levels of how we treat other people and how we form basic family units. In both of these instances, the changes came not because of independent recognition of the need to change, but in response to outside political pressure. Moral change comes when it runs counter to popular pressure, not when it caves into it (even when the popular culture happens to be right, as in both of these instances). Mohandas K. Gandhi and Martin Luther King also led movements that resulted in changes in fundamental moral standards, but they waged their campaigns against the prevailing political and cultural pressures, not caving in to them.

Claims by Mormons that these changes reflected the independent will of the an Eternal God would have much greater credibility if they had been timed so well to social pressure.

9
Christianity and Contemporary Issues

This chapter addresses some of the contemporary political, social and values-based issues often raised by today's conservative "Christians," that are frequently the direct opposite of the teachings attributed to Jesus, including such hot-button issues as abortion, same-sex marriage, preserving the Founders' cherished separation of church and state, the imagined "war on Christmas" (and "war on Christianity" in general) and others. We will examine why Christians take a non-Biblical view that is almost completely opposite of Jesus, and how this came to be.

Is Morality Declining?

A number of those who have written to me assert that, even if I am right, it is dangerous to undermine the literal belief in Christianity because it offers moral stability.

Betrayal of Jesus

They claim that, as a literal belief in Christianity has declined, that modern society has become more immoral.

In many respects, we are actually a more just and moral society than at any time in our history or the history of the world. We no longer practice slavery. We no longer practice child labor or the horrible oppression of assembly lines as they were known a hundred years ago. We protect working people. We protect women and minorities. We encourage those who are disabled to have greater equality of access to opportunities and to participate in the mainstream of everyday life. There is more charity and kindness and giving than ever in history.

While there are clearly some problems that exist, and some of them are new, they are not caused by removing the superficial, trivial symbols from ancient mythologies such as mandating very banal prayers in schools or posting the Ten Commandments. They are caused by a move toward a more impersonal society that results from the urban congestion of mega-cities that did not exist 200 years ago, before the Industrial Revolution. In those days, the infrastructure, communications systems and technology to produce food on farms and keep it fresh for delivery to cities simply did not exist. While a few mega-cities did exist in ancient times (Rome, London, Paris, Beijing), the resources needed to sustain large cities caused that to be a rare, aberrant phenomenon. In 1800 when Thomas Jefferson was President, the largest city in the United States was New York with 60,000 people; second was Philadelphia with 30,000. Today those would be considered small towns. The people who produced goods were personally acquainted with the people who consumed them, their neighbors. The burgeoning crush of congestion and the alienation of those who produce from the strangers that consume creates indifference, which requires regulatory protection. Media and communications allow the rapid spread of new ideas and images (not all of them good) which does more to upset traditional values than outdated mythologies or removing superficial symbols such as a bland, non-sectarian prayer that no one paid attention to anyway.

Along the same lines, many have written me to attest as to how Christianity has improved the quality of their lives. In many cases, I have no doubt but what their brand of Christianity works for them, just as others' brands of Christianity do for them. Buddhism works for others. Judaism for others, and Hinduism, Islam, and so on. Yet not all the details of their factual claims are specifically or actually true. The point is that these are tools to help us steer away from counterproductive wallowing in purely selfish, base desires. If they work to make our lives better, it is not necessarily because they are literally true, but because they provide a sense of values, virtues and purposefulness, as well as an organizational framework within which to express them. In other cases, religion has not led to improved quality of life, but rather to persecution, violence, international strife, etc.

Is Religion Necessary for Morality?

Some claim that it is not possible to have morality apart from religious authority. Such people perpetuate the simplistic myth of morality by externally-imposed fiat — that unless there is an all-powerful authority figure standing over us, threatening to punish us for doing wrong, we will have no reason to be moral.

To say that morality is based on "God" because he has the POWER is to say that morality is based on power. Because god is the biggest, baddest dude in the universe, morality is nothing more than a cosmic game of "might makes right."

Betrayal of Jesus

Cowering in fearful obeisance to dominating bullies is not morality.

The only true morality is that which springs from internalizing self-actualized compassion, the self-driven compulsion to be kind and loving because it makes the world we are a part of a more harmonious place for everyone. It is morality we adhere to even when no one, including imaginary sky gods, is watching.

When parents use the "Big Santa is watching" threat to try to coerce "moral" behavior in children, does that prove anything factually about the existence of Santa? Or merely that those who respond to such externally-imposed "morality" are simply childish?

The key to whether a system of moral teaching (whether religious or otherwise) improves the quality of our lives or makes it more harsh, is whether it promotes love, harmony and positive values.

"Traditional Values"?

One point that needs special emphasis is the way in which modern evangelicals create a specific code of Puritanical "morality," especially in matters of sexuality, and then claim it to represent "traditional" or Biblical values when they bear little, if any, resemblance to sexual standards of the Bible.

Premarital sex: I Cor 7:36 explicitly states that if an unmarried couple have sex before marriage, there is no sin as long as they subsequently do get married. Note that he does not say the sin is "forgiven," but that there *"is no sin"!* Many in modern culture confuse fornication (premarital sex) with adultery (extramarital violatons of the marital vows). They forget that while the penalty for adultery was death by stoning, the penalty for fornication was to marry your partner, well, unless it was one of the same-sex deals.

While this may come as a surprise to many modern Christians following a more recent tradition of neo-Puritan prudery, one must consider that, while Paul (author of the passage) is surely no friend to the Law of Moses, it did reflect conventions regarding sexual morality that he would be familiar with. And according to the Old Testament Law of Moses, in Exodus 22:16, in a chapter that details the penalties for minor offenses, the penalty for a man seducing a virgin is that he must marry her and, if her father refuses to grant permission, he must remit a monetary payment the equivalent of a marriage present for a virgin. In a chapter filled with specific penalties, no other penalty for fornication is specified, whereas the crime of adultery — the violation of vows made — is elsewhere repeatedly accompanied by a mandatory death penalty.

Abortion: Those who claim to oppose abortion based on the Bible are wrong. Although abortion was known and practiced in Bible times, the Bible never says one single word against abortion. The Bible speaks of birth, death, life, pregnancy, and God's foreknowledge of individuals, not only before birth, but before they're even fertilized, or "formed in the womb" (Jeremiah 1:5). Any one of these references would have been a perfect opportunity to explicitly prohibit abortion if any such intent existed, but they did not. The only explicit reference to intentionally terminating a pregnancy is in Numbers 5:12-28 which specifically permits abortion through the Hebrew ritual of Sotah, using an ancient abortifacient of "bitter water" described in the King James version as "ephah of barley meal." The ritual is required in cases where a man suspects that his wife may have been impregnated by another man. According to the Hebrews' superstitions about the ritual of Sotah, if the woman were guilty, the bastard fetus would be expelled (aborted), but would remain safe if she were innocent. While abortion *per se* is not mentioned here or anywhere else in the Bible, the references to Sotah causing "thy high to rot, and thy belly to swell," as well as the "curse" to a woman (the loss of a pregnancy or the barrenness of total infertility), may not be clearly understood by many readers in our time, but would be clearly understood in the era in which it was written and can be interpreted as an instance in which, under specific conditions, the Bible not only *permits* abortion, but *commands* it.

Same-sex marriage: Similarly, the Bible is cited as a basis for opposing homosexuality in general, and same-sex marriage in particular. It is true that the Law of Moses forbids homosexuality (Leviticus 18:22; 20:13), but (as noted in Chapter 3) the same Law also prohibits eating pork and shellfish (Leviticus chapter 11), and requires ritual purification of women completing menstruation, yet these commandments are not so widely cited.

In like vein, conservative "Christians" often describe the sins that supposedly caused god to turn the cities of Sodom and Gomorrah into pillars of salt (Genesis chapter 19) as being references to homosexual relationships. This is purely speculative conjecture on their parts, as the passage in Genesis does not actually say that. And if they really believe the Bible to be without internal contradictions, then their conclusion is explicitly rejected by a much later passage, Ezekiel 16:49-50, which describes the sin of Sodom as being that those who were prideful and of luxurious comforts, but who refused to help those in need, when it says: "Behold, this was this guilt of your sister Sodom: she and her daughters had pride, excess of food, and prosperous ease, but did not aid the poor and needy. They were haughty and did an abomination before me, so I removed them, when I saw it."

The idea that "Traditional Marriage" means "one man and one woman" is not Bible-based at all. According to the Old Testament, the institution of marriage by God is that of one man and multiple prepubescent underage women, who must be of the same ethnicity and are essentially his chattel property, over whom he has "dominion" in the same way as he has over his livestock. There are numerous instances of polygamous marriage in the Old Testament, always reported with approval and never with criticism for the polygamy itself unless it involved other wrongdoing. The Law of Moses explicitly recognizes polygamous marriage and sets forth rules for its governance in Exodus 21:10-11 and Deuteronomy 21:15-17. Isaac, son of Abraham, was given two wives at the same time (sisters Leah and Rachel; Genesis chapter 29). Kings David and Solomon had "many wives" (1 Sam 25:43; I Sam 27:3; I Sam 30:5;18; 2 Sam 5:13; I Chron 14:3; I Kings 11:3 and were only criticized for the foreign wives or when David killed Uriah to take his wife Bathsheba). Hebrew war hero Gideon was acclaimed for his "many wives" (Judges 8:30), and various other Israelites were celebrated for multiple marriages (I Sam 1:2; I Kings 20:5; 1 Chron 4:5; 2 Chron 11:21; 2 Chron 13:21; 2 Chron 24:3). And this is only a small sampling of the total number of favorable references to polygamy in the Old Testament.

The "Traditional Values" movement seems to be very selective as to which "Biblical" traditions they honor.

Could an All-knowing, All-powerful, All-loving God Allow Suffering of the Innocent?

Often we hear accounts of those who suffer from terrible illnesses and afflictions which they did nothing to bring upon themselves and which they did nothing to deserve. Or we hear of the innocent victims of torture, cruelty, enslavement, criminal violence or terrorism. We hear of how God was in the towers with the victims of the World Trade Center terror attacks of September 11, 2001.

But how could a god who is supposed to be all-knowing, all-powerful and all-loving allow suffering by those who are completely innocent?

So again, where was God? I don't mean in the aftermath of courageous heroes or compassion for victims. The valor of heroes and the suffering of victims has nothing to do with God. Where was God *before* the planes crashed?

If a supervising adult were watching kids playing in the pool, and clearly saw as one child held another's head underwater, how would we judge the adult who simply stood by and watched as one child forcibly, maliciously and intentionally drowned another, taking no action to intervene? I can assure you, the excuse that the responsible adult was just allowing the child to exercise his or her "free will" would not be received very kindly. If fallible mortal humans — who do not claim to be all-knowing, all-powerful or all-loving, but merely *more*-knowing, *more*-powerful and *more*-loving than children or the uncivilized — are morally accountable for protective intervention, then it is logically impossible to simultaneously believe that God is all-knowing, that God is all-powerful, and that God is all-righteous and loving.

As some survivors thank God for sparing their lives, how must the families feel of those who God didn't care enough to save?

Yes, yes, I understand that the traditional response is to say that God allowed the terrorists to murder thousands of innocent civilians and heroic firefighters and police because our "Heavenly Father" grants his children, the terrorists, their "free will." Forgive me, however, if I then ask you, again, that if the parent supervising the children's pool party, stood by and watched, in full view and knowledge, as one child intentionally and maliciously drowned another, and did nothing to intervene, would this be excused by you as allowing the child his "free will"? If you do not allow this standard for the parent, how can you allow it for God who, if anything, should be held to a higher standard?

At least those who believe in "higher powers" in the universe that are merely "higher" or "superior" and not fully "omnipotent" or "supreme" can say that their less-than-omni gods are just doing the imperfect best that they can.

Christmas and Make-believe "Culture Wars"

In recent years, the myth of a "War on Christmas" has been fabricated by conservative "Christians" as a pretext for stirring up defensive animosity toward those who resist their efforts at dominating all of culture and society. This is seen in several specific ways:

Happy Holidays

One of the most visible manifestations of the paranoia behind these fabricated fears about "culture wars" is a campaign to replace the generic holiday season greeting of "Happy Holidays" with the more narrow, specific greeting of "Merry Christmas," regardless of whether or not the recipient even celebrates that holiday.

Those who are consumed by such delusions fail to understand the perspective of those who say, "Happy Holidays" to strangers during the period between mid-November and mid-January, when a number of holidays occur including Thanksgiving, Hanukkah, Solstice, Yule, Christmas, Kwanzaa, New

Betrayal of Jesus

Year, Epiphany and, in some years, Ramadan and/or the Feasts of Eid al-Adha and Al-Hijra. Some of these holidays represent religious or cultural viewpoints; some are secular. But they all occur during this time of year. And when you meet a stranger, not knowing their viewpoint, saying "Happy Holidays" is simply a gesture of respect to avoid judging others or imposing your choices on them.

If I encounter someone and do not know the person's preference, I find it least presumptious to say "Happy Holidays"; if I do know their preference, then I will offer the appropriate greeting. If I know someone celebrates Christmas — as I do — I will greet them with "Merry Christmas."

There is no anti-Christian bias; there is no "War on Christmas." These myths are the creations of those seeking to stir up hatred where there is none, in a season meant to represent "peace on earth, goodwill to all."

The "Reason for the Season"

One of the common sentiments expressed by conservative Christians regarding the holiday season is that, "Jesus is the reason for the season."

This is not true.

The *season* in which Christmas (and many other holidays) falls is **winter**.

The "reason for the *season*" is the Winter Solstice.

The date of Jesus' birth is unknown. The date of the Christmas holiday, and many of the traditions of the Christmas season (trees, lights, Yule logs, evergreen berries such as holly, Father Winter and elves) are all ***pagan*** in origin, and reflect the fact that many holidays are placed in this ***season*** to celebrate the lengthening of days and the hope of renewal.

Jesus was born into a province of the Roman Empire, on a date lost to history. December 25 of the Julian calendar was already established as the biggest holiday of the Roman calendar: the pagan holiday "Saturnalia." Even in modern astrology (which originated in that era) Saturn "rules" the sign of Capricorn, which begins with the winter solstice.

Saturnalia was a drunken bacchanal of orgies and earthly pleasures, the biggest holiday of the Roman Empire. It was not observed by the early faithful Christians. After Constantine, when Rome officially became Christian, the Church/State combination had two problems:

1: The people did not want to give up their biggest holiday, any more than people like me who are raised Christian but go in different directions want to give up our holidays or traditions; and

2: The Church was beginning to set aside holy days for saints and wanted a holy day for the biggest star of all — not a mere saint but the *son of god,* Jesus Christ, but had no idea when his birthday was, though they suspected it to be most likely in spring.

How to consolidate these two concerns?

Not knowing the actual date of Jesus' birth, but needing a date on which to celebrate it, the church decided to pick an arbitrary date to assign as Jesus' birthday, and they picked December 25 so they could replace the pagan bacchanal of Saturnalia — the biggest of all Roman holidays — with what would then become the biggest of all Christian holy days (holidays).

As Christianity spread and merged with other cultures, they blended the Christian traditions with local traditions from local pagan celebrations, including such things as Father Winter (Santa Claus), holly, evergreen trees, elves, and still some leftover revelry and drunkeness from the old Saturnalia.

Christmas was here before Jesus, and while the addition of the Christian tradition is one important component of Christmas, the holiday still goes on with or without him.

Jesus is *not* the "reason for the *season,*" and Christmas is but one of many holidays celebrated during this season.

Christmas did not originate with Jesus, nor did most of the other pagan traditions of this holiday. Not only are there many other holidays during this *season,* but even Christmas itself originates from a ***pagan*** holiday, and many of the traditions added later (trees, lights, Yule logs, evergreen berries such as holly, Father Winter and elves) are incorporated from other pagan traditions from all over the world.

Jesus vs. Santa Claus

To self-described "Christians," the holiday of Christmas revolves around the person of Jesus and the occasion of his birth. For many of those Christians, the figure of Santa Claus is a close second, and for many non-Christians who celebrate Christmas as something other than a religious observance, Santa is the primary figure.

The two have much in common.

Both Jesus and Santa Claus are based on real persons (Jesus of Nazareth, son of a carptenter, and St. Nicholas, Bishop of Myra in Asia Minor in the 4th Century) who likely existed, but for whom absolute verification is greatly lacking. Based on the most reliable information, both were simple, kindly gentlemen who had an appreciation for the needs of children and the individual worth of each child. Beyond the sketchy (and unverified) details of their lives, there are many myths and legends and exaggerations, often invoking miracles and magic.

The two are both excellent figureheads for representing various dimensions of a special holiday, as long as we remember to separate reality from fantasy as to both (more about the reality and fantasy of the Santa Claus myth in the introduction to Chapter 10).

Religion and Science; Religion in Education

We hear about calls for "balance" by religious extremists, who demand that, in matters when science and superstition clash, we need to "teach the controversy," as if to say there is equal merit balancing on a scale of knowledge gained through peer-reviewed scientific methodology and protocols, and superstitions handed down by fiat from ancient primitive tribal societies.

In 1491, the vast majority of humans on the earth, owing largely what was taught in their religious dogma, believed that the earth was flat and that the sun, moon and stars revolved around a stationary earth that was at the center of the universe.

Yet in the world of science, those views were challenged and, when those challenges arose, they were seen as heretical and, at the very least, controversial. As far back as the year 240 BC — a full 1,732 years before Columbus set sail and proved with certainty the spherical nature of the earth — science had known that the world was spherical, *and had accurately computed its correct size,* based on the work of Eratosthenes in ancient Greece. Yet the work of this pagan was rejected outright until the proof was so overwhelming, and then the Church changed its views and took advantage of new discoveries to engage in new conquests.

Betrayal of Jesus

At one time, as Galileo and Copernicus can attest, any challenge to the idea of a heliocentric solar system or the earth revolving around the sun, was to risk being branded a heretic and put at risk of one's life or at least one's freedom.

Today, even the most ardent believers in religion with only a few fringe holdouts, have conceded that, yes, a spherical earth revolves around a heliocentric solar system, and they no longer demand that we reject these scientific certainties or even that we "teach the [former] controversies."

In contrast, in more recent subjects of scientific inquiry such as biology and paleoanthropology, those who base their beliefs on ancient myths and legends, reject more recent scientific advances, and demand that their myths of Creationism (the belief that God created all things specifically, also known as "Intelligent Design") be taught in science classes alongside Evolution — that as long as large numbers of people believe in such ancient legends, however little objective, factual basis may exist to support them — that we need to "teach the controversy."

The problem is that Creationism, even if dressed up with the fancy title "Intelligent Design," is not science. Science, however imperfect and incomplete, is based on specific protocols of empirical, measurable, quantifiable, replicable observation and experimentation — observable, measurable, replicably quantifiable data such as transitional fossils, including those between major branches on the tree of life such as from reptiles to birds, as well as specific verification of relationships based on the kind of highly-reliable DNA evidence that can convict the guilty, free the innocent or establish paternity with absolute certainty. No one who accepts DNA evidence in a criminal case or paternity suit can question the validity of the same DNA that confirms relationships among differing species.

In contrast, *faith* is not based on any such observation or objective evidence. The very definition of faith in the Bible is that "faith is the substance of things hoped for, the evidence of things *not seen."* [Hebrews 11:1; emphasis added]. That which is *not seen* cannot, by definition, be part of a systematic protocol of *observation.*

Creationism or "Intelligent Design" is simply not based on science. There is no "controversy" to be taught in any scientific sense of the word. The Creation mythology demanded by religious conservatives (who would reject calls to teach the creation myths of other ancient peoples) is based on the story in Genesis, although as we have seen in Chapter 3 that there are two different accounts of Creation in Genesis, and the account in Genesis Chapter One directly contradicts that in Genesis Chapter Two.

Creationists always demand "perfection" of science, which (unlike dogma) acknowledges that it is the work of fallible, imperfect humans and is always, well, "evolving" towards more complete knowledge and greater accuracy, but will never attain perfection, while at least backing up its claims with peer-reviewed, objective evidence from scientific methods and protocols. In contrast, the same Creationists who demand that imperfect science live up to the infallible standard they claim for themselves, have never once offered the slightest shred of objective, replicable, observable, peer-reviewed evidence for a talking snake in a magic garden who convinced a woman made from her husband's rib to eat an enchanted fruit that God planted in their garden and then forbade them from eating.

Betrayal of Jesus

There may be a place for religious teachings in schools, as literature, or for its role in the development of what became the discipline of theology, or in legitimate discussions of comparative theology — but not in science classes.

It always strikes me as humorous that the same people who demand "balance" in biology and geology classes never demand the same balance in medical schools by hiring medicine men or other quacks, or in astronomy classes by teaching astrology (which is actually based on the ancient Greek theological belief that the sun, moon and planets were literally Gods in the sky, each assigned an area of influence over various aspects of the lives of mortals, reflected in "signs" that reflected the season of one's birth and "houses" that reflected the time of one's birth, thus recognizing the earth's revolution around the sun as well as its daily rotation on its axis). Nor does the Bible literalists' demand for "balance" ever go both ways. They never demand that the creation myths of other primitives be taught alongside their own, nor have they ever provided quantifiable, replicable *scientific* data to support their creation accounts from Genesis.

Religion and Politics

Is the United States a "Christian Nation"?
There is no doubt that George Washington, Sam Adams, John Adams and many others among the Founding Fathers were devoutly religious (although Washington's attendance at services was notoriously spotty).

There is also no doubt that Benjamin Franklin, Alexander Hamilton, Thomas Jefferson, James Madison and Thomas Paine were clearly not devout Christians, though they came out of that background and later developed their own independent thoughts that rejected both the literal belief in an inerrant/infallible Bible as well as a rejection of most tenets of traditional Christian dogma. Thomas Paine was especially hostile toward traditional religion. In his 1794 treatise, "The Age of Reason," he wrote: "Whenever we read the obscene stories, the voluptuous debaucheries, the cruel and torturous executions, the unrelenting vindictiveness, with which more than half the Bible is filled, it would be more consistent that we called it the word of a demon than the Word of God. It is a history of wickedness that has served to corrupt and brutalize mankind; and for my own part, I sincerely detest it, as I detest everything that is cruel."

Jefferson, a self-described "Deist" (believing in a "higher power" as "Prime Cause" in the universe but without ongoing involvement with its subsequent course) appreciated the more liberal teachings of Jesus but rejected his literal divinity or the miracles of the Bible, or its god-given inerrancy. He had especially harsh words towards Paul, whom he described as "the first corruptor of the doctrines of Jesus." [Letters to William Short, April 13, 1820 and James Smith, December 8, 1822]

Even among those who claimed some degree of religious devotion and belief, there does not appear to be any evidence that they wanted to impose it on others or bring it into the public square. These early leaders were highly suspicious of government, and those who were believers did not trust government to be making choices about religion while those who were not religious certainly saw no role for the government in promoting something they did not believe in.

Thus they created a Constitution and Bill of Rights in which the separation of church from state was the first among the enumerated rights and, while that phrase itself does not appear in the Constitution (it comes from a 1802 letter by

Betrayal of Jesus

Thomas Jefferson to the Baptist Church of Danbury, Connecticut), the "Freedom of Religion" in the First Amendment has been universally interpreted by legal authorities as being able to choose ones own religious *or non-religious* path.

There is no mention of Jesus or Christianity in the Declaration of Independence. There are only generalized references to the "Laws of Nature" and to "Nature's God" or "Divine Providence" — nothing remotely specific to the Christian belief system, which its author, Thomas Jefferson, did not believe in. These benign, general references seem stylistic in the same sense that we might refer to "Mother Nature" or "Father Time" without pronouncing a literal belief in them. And there is no mention whatsoever of religion at all in the original Constitution, except to prohibit any religious requirement for holding office (Section VI), nor in the Amendments to the Constitution, other than the First Amendment which requires complete religious freedom.

Some additional expressions by Thomas Jefferson as to his personal lack of belief in Christian dogma and the separation between church and state:

From "Notes on the State of Virginia" 1782: "I have examined all the known superstitions of the world, and I do not find in our particular superstition of Christianity one redeeming feature. They are all alike founded on fables and mythology. Millions of innocent men, women and children, since the introduction of Christianity, have been burnt, tortured, fined and imprisoned. What has been the effect of this coercion? To make one half of the world fools and the other half hypocrites; to support roguery and error all over the earth."

From "Notes on the State of Virginia" 1782: "The legitimate powers of government extend to such acts only as are injurious to others. But it does me no injury for my neighbor to say there are twenty gods, or no god."

From a letter to John Adams dated April 11, 1823: "The day will come when the mystical generation of Jesus, by the supreme being as his father in the womb of a virgin will be classed with the fable of the generation of Minerva in the brain of Jupiter."

From a letter to Dr. Thomas Cooper dated February 10, 1814: "Christianity neither is, nor ever was a part of the common law."

From a letter to Horatio G. Spafford dated March 17, 1814: "In every country and in every age, the priest has been hostile to liberty. He is always in alliance with the despot, abetting his abuses in return for protection to his own."

From a letter to Francis Adrian Van Der Kemp dated July 30, 1816: "No man ever had a distinct idea of the Trinity. It is the mere abracadabra of the mountebanks calling themselves the priests of Jesus."

From a letter to Correa de Serra dated April 11, 1820: "Priests ... dread the advance of science as witches do the approach of daylight."

Even John Adams, who most certainly was a devout believer as a matter of his own personal, individual conscience, separated personal beliefs from public policy. In terms of official policy, Adams was firmly with those who kept god out of the picture. Here is the official language from the Treaty of Tripoli of 1797, negotiated and signed by *John Adams,* and ratified *unanimously* by the U.S. Senate without debate: "The government of the United States of America is *not, in any sense, founded on the Christian religion."* [Emphasis added]

Betrayal of Jesus

As a postscript, it should also be noted that Abraham Lincoln also expressed rather candid views. While not one of the original Founders, he is credited with saving the Republic at a time of its greatest crisis, and is considered one of our greatest presidents. In a letter dated Sept 13, 1862 to Judge J.S. Wakefield after death of his son Willie, Lincoln said: "My earlier views of the unsoundness of the Christian scheme of salvation and the human origin of the scriptures, have become clearer and stronger with advancing years and I see no reason for thinking I shall ever change them. The Bible is not my book nor Christianity my profession."

As noted earlier, I see today a resurgence of those who seek to unravel the carefully crafted separation of church and state that was the genius of our Founders, and which enhanced the integrity of both church and state. I see many conservative Christians trying to create an official religion in our secular nation. They do not have confidence that others will be attracted to their brand of harsh, cruel Christian teaching rooted in Paul rather than Jesus on its own merits, but that it requires authoritarian government coercion to force itself onto others. Ironically, the same conservatives who express little confidence in the government to handle other matters are quite content to let government dictate matters of faith; they seem to place more trust in the government to decide matters of conscience than in their churches, families and private religious schools. It is incumbent on all free people to resist the intursion of public institutions into the most private of personal domains. The last time the Church dominated the Western world, we called it the Dark Ages. Today, many of those with the same mentality seek to resist and obstruct science and reason and return us to that era of dark reliance on superstition. It is hoped that this effort can help expose some of the reasons why such primivitve thinking must be rejected.

Who Do You Trust? Church Leaders or Politicians?

Jesus taught in his seminal public discourse, the Sermon on the Mount, that religious exercises such as prayer and worship should be personal and private. On prayer, Jesus did not suggest, he *commanded* in Matthew 5:5 "thou shalt not" pray in public. Not even in the synagogues or street corners! How can anyone who calls themselves "Christians" lobby for public prayers? Have they even read the Bible that they proclaim to be the Word of God?

And Jesus clearly delineated between religious authority and the secular, non-religious authority of the government. Jesus makes it explicitly clear in Matt 22:21 and Mark 12:17 and Luke 20:25 that we should render to the government (Caesar) that which is the government's (Caesar's), and separately to God that which is God's. In this way, we can see that Jefferson's vision of a "wall of separation between church and state," an expression he was the first to use while writing a letter explaining this concept to the Baptist Association of Danbury, Connecticut, in 1802.

Would Jesus Be Liberal or Conservative?

Labels such as "liberal" and "conservative" and especially partisan identities such as Democrat or Republican did not exist at the time Jesus lived on this earth. Carefully thought out political and economic philosophies such as capitalism or socialism had not been contemplated. So clearly no party or ideology can unequivocally claim Jesus as an adherent. However, if one considers the teachings attributed to Jesus in the gospels, and compares them to modern philosophies, he would clearly fall into the liberal camp.

Look at some of these specific teachings:

On rich and poor: "Sell all your possess and give to the poor." (Mark 10:21). Or: "It is easier for a camel to go through the eye of a needle, than for a rich man to enter into the kingdom of God." (Matt 19:23-24; Mark 10:25; Luke 18:25).

For those who oppose higher tax rates on higher levels of income: "From everyone who has been given much, much will be required; and to whom they entrusted much, of him they will ask all the more." (Luke 12:48).

Jesus followers took him seriously: "All that believed were together, and had all things in common; and sold their possessions and goods, and parted them to all men, according to their needs." (Acts 2:44-45; emphasis added; this was enforced by threat of death as recounted in a more detailed description in Acts 4:32-37 and Acts 5:1-11). If someone were to suggest such a practice today, those who claim to be Jesus' followers today would call him a Communist. Would they call Jesus a Communist? A Socialist?.

So if Jesus is such an outspoken liberal, why do those who claim to be his followers stake out a conservative position so opposite of what he taught?

It all goes back to that fundamental conflict that has been repeatedly cited in earlier chapters between Jesus (supported by his brother James) and the renegade "apostle" Paul.

Jesus is compassionate (some might ridicule him as a "bleeding heart" liberal) and inclusive; Paul is the one who oppresses gays, women and slaves. Jesus is flexible and understanding; Paul is rigid, legalistic, strict, dogmatic and doctrinaire.

Jesus teaches salvation through universal compassionate love expressed actively through actions; Paul teaches an easy, selfish salvation based on expressing belief, and says it doesn"t matter what you do, and bases this teaching on a doctrine rooted in a bloody ritual of human sacrifice.

"What if You're Wrong?"

Many times, in written correspondence or one-on-one dialogue, when Christians become frustrated with their inability to reconcile their mythological literalism with a more expansive and more realistic perspective on Christianity, they will respond with a statement that goes something like this: "You had better be sure that you are right. If I'm wrong, all I've sacrificed is a little inconvenience. But if *you're* wrong, you'll pay for your error by spending eternity in hell."

This statement is a colloquialized adaptation of an idea postulated by the French mathematician and philosopher Blaise Pascal.* As a mathematician, he earned famed for developing early theories of probability applicable in games of chance. He asserts that the infinite magnitude of God is so vast that it is incomprehensible to mortal humans, and being beyond our capacity for understanding certainly exceeds our capacity to prove or disprove. Thus he claims we must either believe or not believe based on faith or the lack of it. In weighing this decision, since we can't resort to logic or proof, since it is beyond us, we must find some other rationale. So he likens it to a wager in which there are two choices: either we accept God or reject belief in deity. As a wager, he finds this a no-brainer. If you believe and you are right, you have infinite, eternal gain of infinite, eternal happiness; if you are wrong you have suffered minimal loss, if any, and probably still had a better quality of life. On the other hand, if you

---

* Blaise Pascal lived from 1623 to 1662. This example is taken from a treatise called "The Wager" from his writings of *Pensees* (or *Thoughts)*.

disbelieve and are right, you could avail of more enjoyment of vices (which might actually not be a better quality of life); but if you are wrong you have risked everything and lost your eternal reward and instead suffer eternal damnation. So the risk on 50/50 odds is a choice between infinite gain with minimal (if any) loss versus minimal (if any) gain with risk of infinite loss.

But no matter its lofty philosophical origins, ultimately the claim is reduced to what it really is: an empty, meaningless exercise in frustration. It is a hollow "cosmic death threat." And when looked at from another perspective, even Christians can readily see its fallacy. This point is further discussed in Chapter 10.

When I was in high school back in the 1960s, I had a very close friend who was a very devout Sunni Moslem from Egypt. At that time I was still a zealous Christian, active in youth ministries. It was at his urging that I first read a translation of the Koran, and we spent many enjoyable lunch hours debating our respective religious perspectives. He used to say something very similar to me: "What if you're wrong?" And I would say the same thing back to him. And neither of us was the slightest bit intimidated by the others' threats, which are merely a substitute for the failure to come up with a more substantial, logical basis for discussion.

Similarly, even within Christianity, differing branches of Christians say the same thing to each other. Differing sects of evangelical Protestants may argue about points of doctrine, but generally accept the legitimacy of each other's claims of having been "saved" by "accepting Jesus Christ as Savior." However these evangelical Protestants generally will *not* accept the validity of other Christian branches such as liberal Christians, Catholics, Mormons or Jehovah's Witnesses, all of whom they claim are not real Christians despite all of them having built their doctrines around a messianic belief in Jesus as divine savior. Similarly, Catholics, Mormons, and Jehovah's Witnesses, each of which claim a monopoly on the truth, say the same thing to all the others.

Without additional basis for why each of their claims should be accepted as the one and only valid claim, the mere utterance of this "cosmic death threat" means nothing.

I have shown with ample evidence that the literal claims of divinity for the Bible and for Christian mythology, whatever other importance and merit they definitely offer, are the works of wise but ancient men, not of any divine deity. In basing these claims on solid foundations of support, I have no more fear or intimidation from such hollow threats because I do not accept Jesus as a literal atoning sacrifice than I do because I also do not accept Zeus, Jupiter, or the gods of ancient Egyptians, Incas or Mayans as being literally divine (though I also find much wisdom and value in those ancient mythologies).

Personal Witness

Many Christians write to affirm that their belief is not just based on logic, but rather on a "personal relationship with Jesus Christ" — that their hearts have been touched and inspired as a witness to the truth of their beliefs.

Such testimonies are indeed powerful. I know, because I felt the same deep and passionate conviction back when I was a Christian.

But again, this experience proves nothing because it is not unique to Christianity. On the contrary, it is common to almost all religions. This deeply personal feeling is the essence of the religious experience, and is what motivates and drives those who become the most devout and ardent adherents to any sect. This is what inspires martyrs to be willing to give up their mortal lives for their faith, whether they be Catholics fighting Protestants in Ireland or Jews and Moslems fighting each other in the Middle East. All of them are passionate in their fervent devotion because they have all had the same experience — except that the same experience "proved" very differing conclusions to very differing religious communities.

Religion is a powerful force in many lives, and many have had powerful experiences that engender strong belief, but this is a phenomenon exhibited in all faiths. Therefore, since they cannot all be true, such experiences may be powerful, but they do not validate claims of the supernatural.

10

Is There a God?

When I contemplate the question, "Is there a God?" I hear echoes of an innocent, doe-eyed child looking up and asking, "Is there a Santa Claus."

In its childlike naïveté, which is endearing for the child but simplistic for adults, the child envisions a specific, real, tangible jolly old man who magically fills all the Christmas stockings in the world in a single night (without considering that [most] Jewish, Islamic, Hindu, Buddhist and atheist children are not included).

The adult may respond truthfully that there "is" a Santa Claus, but may mean something far less literal than the child's youthful and imaginative expectations. So, echoing the words and spirit of Francis Parcellus Church to young Virginia O'Hanlon, "Yes, Virginia, there is a God."

However, it is not the middle eastern monotheistic [simultaneously triune?] sky god of scriptural mythology nor is it the anthropomorphic deity in whose image the legend says we were created.

Betrayal of Jesus

Is there intelligence and energy in the universe greater than that of humans? I hope so!

Is there energy and power greater than that of humans? No doubt.

Is there something that was here before everything else? Well, something had to be first. In the interchangeability of matter and energy, was matter/energy first expressed as matter or energy? When and how did consciousness emerge out of non-consciousness matter/energy?

Is it OK, if one does not know the answer to any of these questions, to say "I don't know" instead of feeling compelled to concoct an answer?

So: Yes, Virginia, there is a God.

—

In this book, we have shown with certainty that it is possible to prove that specific religious claims can be shown to be in error, such as claims of infallibility and inerrancy of scriptures that can be shown to be demonstrably fallible and errant, based on internal contradictions and inconsistencies or the fact that prophecies of specific events failed to occur within the time periods specified for their completion.

But what about more general claims about the underlying concepts on which religion itself is based?

But what about claims for the existence of God himself? (Or herself or itself?)

Can we, by reason, logic and evidence alone, disprove with certainty the existence of a supreme (or at least superior) being?

In terms of examining earlier philosophical claims about the existence of a deity or higher power, will assume the reader has some degree of familiarity with them. Many advanced theories claiming to prove or disprove the existence of God take entire books to present in full, and have generated additional whole books of discussion about them. It is not the purpose of this brief review to try to explain them in full to someone not familiar with them, beyond a cursory summary to provide just enough information to address the basic ideas.

Traditional Rationalizations for God and Counterarguments

Throughout the centuries, there have been various efforts to prove logically the existence of a supreme being, or "God."

St. Anselm's Ontological Argument

The Claim: St. Anselm: "Proslogion" The Ontological Argument first published in the 1070's. St. Anselm asserts that theists (believers) and atheists (non-believers) both agree that the concept of god is that god represents the highest (most perfect) representation of "good." A real-world manifestation is a higher level of good, i.e., it would be something more "perfect" than the mere idea of a concept of what is most perfect; therefore, the mere idea or concept of the highest representation of perfection would not, itself, be the most perfect. Since both the theist and atheist agree on the concept of the highest representation of perfection, but only disagree as to its existence in the real world, but a real world manifestation would be more perfect than a non-existent concept of what is most perfect, the idea of a non-existent highest representation is an inherently contradictory concept and is therefore impossible; therefore a "most perfect" being must necessarily exist in the real world.

Why it Fails: The claim fails for several reasons:

1. Theists and atheists do **not** agree on the concept of god as being the highest representation of perfection. There are many different concepts of what a deity would entail, and not all embody absolute perfection, which many nonbelievers assert is not possible either in the real world or even as a concept, which humans are not able to conceive. Neither theists nor atheists have a true idea or concept of a "most perfect being." They have a label, or an idealized abstraction, but not the concept or idea itself, because deity (if the highest manifestation of absolute perfection) is infinite and cannot be grasped conceptually in the finite minds of mortal humans. If it can be brought within the limited scope of finite mortals' ability to conceive, then it is *not infinite;* it is finite and could always be expanded. The concept that a highest manifestation of absolute perfection exists is not, itself, either the reality or the concept of that highest manifestation.

2. The fundamental premise is flawed. Manifestations in the physical world are *not* more perfect than thoughts about them. Physical representations are always constrained by the finite limitations of the physical world, whereas thoughts are *not subject to any such constraints.* Ultimately, all perceptions, even if they originate from the physical world, are perceived or experienced as non-physical, non-constrained perceptions — sensations converted as experience into thoughts or ideas. St. Anselm offers the example of a painting, claiming that looking at an actual painting is a higher manifestation than the *idea* of the painting. But this is not necessarily true. The physical painting is *not* necessarily more perfect than the *idea* of the painting. Blemishes, brush strokes, inaccuracies of artistic skill of the painter, etc., may be visible in a physical object of art constrained by physical limitations. But in the mind there are no such limits. One can conceive in

Is There A God

three-dimensional representations, and can imagine an object that is entirely free of any blemishes or imperfections whatsoever, in a way that would be impossible in the purely physical dimension. One could also argue that this perfect deity, itself, is spiritual energy rather than physical matter, rendering St. Anselm's argument not only a rational failure, but perhaps even blasphemous.

3. The whole idea that there is something that is the ultimate highest representation of absolute perfection is not logical. It implies some kind of "intrinsic maximum" — that there is some point at which ultimate perfection exists or is even possible. If there is a god, and if we can actually conceive "it," then what happens if "it" creates a new world or does another blessed deed? Has it increased its goodness? Become "better," or "more" perfect? But it was already at the highest maximum perfection, how could it ever add to that? The answer is that the assumption of a "highest" absolute standard of perfection does not exist (which also goes back to the first point — non-believers might *not* even agree on the concept of a highest perfection). We inherently understand this in math or in space/time. There is no end to numbers; you can always add one more. There is no end to space or time; you can always go further away in space or time. These things are infinite. If one believes in an *infinite* supreme being then, by definition, they have also negated St. Anselm's premise that even the theists believe there exists a highest maximum standard of perfection, which is an inherent contradiction to the infinite deity.

Blaise Pascal's Wager

The Claim: Blaise Pascal: "The Wager" (from "Pensées" or "Thoughts") was published after his death in 1662. Pascal's Wager is not really so much a claim to "prove" the existence of God as it is an attempt to show that the odds are more practical for belief in a supreme being than not to believe. It can be summarized as saying, "If you believe in god and are wrong, you lose nothing. If you don't believe in god and are wrong, you suffer the consequences for the rest of eternity. Do you really want to take that bet (wager)?" It is so often thrown in the face of non-believers as a justification for why they should believe that it merits discussion here, as I also addressed it in Chapter 9.

Why it Fails: Pascal, a reformed gambler and mathematical expert on probabilities, treats this as an either/or proposition, with a 50/50 risk on a choice between infinite gain with minimal (if any) loss versus minimal (if any) gain with risk of infinite loss. But in reality, this is not "either/or." There are thousands of belief options. Just within Christianity, you can believe or not believe in Evangelical Protestantism, Liberal ("social gospel") Protestantism, Catholicism, Mormonism, Jehovah's Witness teachings, and others. Then there is Judaism. And there are those Moslems who say you chose to "believe" but you're still consigned to the eternal flames of "fireboarding" in hell because you didn't choose their version of Allah, their holy book Koran (Qur'an) or their prophet (Mohammed). Then there are the kinder, gentler pagan, polytheistic and/or Deist religions whose beliefs are about a deity who doesn't get his/her/its/their feelings hurt so much just because you don't believe in him/her/it/them.

Moreover, the proposition is not 50/50. While certainty or proof for or against the existence of a supreme deity exceeds the capacity of human perception and is not provable, certain specific claims are. And some of the claims that can absolutely be proven with great certainty are to disprove the claims of those Christians who claim the infallibility of an inerrant Bible, since the existence of numerous internal contradictions, factual errors and specific failed prophecies render it not to be inerrant or infallible.

Christians have asked me many times if I don't experience fear about rejecting Jesus Christ as my Lord and Savior. And I ask them if they have any fear in rejecting Allah, Zeus, Jupiter or the gods of the ancient Egyptians, Incas or Mayans as being literally true (though I do note that many of them seem to hedge their bets somewhat by peeking every morning at their printed horoscopes, which are directly rooted in ancient Greek religion).

I am sure that some of my current beliefs are wrong, just as others in the past turned out to be, such as my previous belief in an inerrant/infallible Bible or the bloody human sacrifice mythology of atonement until I found clear and precise evidence to the contrary. But just because some of my beliefs turn out to be wrong, that does not mean that a specific alternative (such as yours) is right, because there are many other alternatives. When I was a high school student back in the 60's, I had a very good friend who was a Moslem from Egypt. We used to debate religion during lunch (I was a devout Christian at that time). He used to say the same thing, "But what if you are wrong?" Does that implied threat frighten you? No? Well neither does yours frighten me. Especially since I know that when someone else has nothing more to offer than these childish threats of a "cosmic death penalty," it means they have nothing of substance to bring to the discussion.

Since every other alternative can say this, that line of thinking does not support any specific alternative. You have to find evidence that supports your positive assertions as well as evidence that refutes the evidence that shows you to be mistaken (however sincere and well-intended you may be).

Betrayal of Jesus

Some have faith in Jesus as the Messiah (or in Paul's distortion of who and what Jesus was). And others' faith is Mohammad, or in Hinduism or Buddhism. Theirs is just as strong, and perhaps has less exposure to contradiction (though it still has some) since the former was written by a single writer and the others do not have the singularly-claimed canonical "word of God." If you are going to make a competing claim based on exactly the same basis, then you are going to have to find some reason to distinguish the validity of yours.

Aristotle's First Cause

The Claim: Cosmological Argument: First Cause; Prime Mover. This is the argument for a higher power first posited by Plato in "The Laws, (Book X)" and "Timaeus" — that the universe could not come into existence by "self-originated motion" to set and maintain motion, and that nothing can be created "ex nihilo" or "out of nothing." The argument was further taken up and expanded by Aristotle in "Metaphysics" and it was Aristotle who coined the term, which is usually translated as "Prime Mover" or "First Cause."

The argument essentially says that nothing can exist by itself. If you see a watch, there had to be a watchmaker. If you see a universe, there had to be a universe maker.

Why it Fails: In establishing causes of things, you can say the watch was created by the watchmaker, and he was created by his parents, and they by theirs, back to the first humans, and the first humans were created by...? We can't see that far back so we don't have clear evidence who created them. But they had to be created by someone or some thing; we just don't know what it was.

But then, something had to create that, and so on, *ad infinitum,* until you get to Aristotle's Prime Mover or First

Cause, who becomes the "higher power" or deified as "God" (or, for the Greeks, "Gods" plural). The problem becomes a circular argument. If something cannot exist without having been created, then how did the Prime Mover get there? Why is this "First Cause" exempt from the basic assumption? But *something* had to exist first! So those who object to the "Prime Mover" say, why not just cut out the middleman, for whom there no corroborating evidence exists, and just say that the Universe, or the "Big Bang," is what came first?

Objection to Belief in Deity and Counterargument

Absence of Evidence

The biggest single objection to belief in the existence of a supreme (or at least superior) creative force in the Universe is the lack of any positive reason for such a belief. Just as you cannot prove that there are no fairies hidden in the thick clouds of Venus, thriving on heat and carbon dioxide, or that there are not two-headed quasi-anthropomorphic space creatures living on planets beyond our galaxy, or one cannot disprove the existence of powerful deities represented by the Sun, Moon and Planets that formed the core of Greek mythology (that were once believed seriously be literally true and which still form the basis for belief in the "influences" of those celestial forces in astrology), so one cannot prove that there is no deity. Thus, the objection is that, if there is no more positive reason to believe in a god than in fairies or space creatures or the deities of ancient mythology, then lacking any reason for such a belief, it is more feasible to reject such belief.

"Absence of evidence is not evidence of absence." But absence of evidence *is* absence of evidence. And in the absence of positive reasons to believe in something that is not made evident by empirical evidence, it is more plausible not to believe in something not evidenced (the simpler explanation) than to believe in something (more complex explanation) for which there is no evidence.

However, the claim that there is *no* reason to believe in a supreme (or superior) being — that there is a complete "absence of evidence" — is questionable.

I have often heard it compared to a child's belief in Santa Claus. It is impossible to absolutely disprove that somewhere in the Universe a Santa Claus does not exist, but the inability to disprove it doesn't make it so, yet we could all agree that it is not a "50/50" equal probability for or against the existence of a Santa Claus.

Yet we should also agree that, in fact, the child does have good reason to believe in Santa Claus. He wakes up Christmas morning and there is a pile of presents. He innately understands that they did not just get there by themselves (something akin to understanding the argument of Prime Cause). Moreover, trusted authorities (parents) who have generally been proved to be reliable, assure him that *they* didn't put the presents there and further assure him that the identity of the gift-giver is known, and it is Santa Claus. It is not at all unreasonable for a small child to therefore accept this as credible evidence.

Further, even when the details of the ruse become known, *the child's basic assumption was valid.* The giver of the gifts was not Santa Claus, but still they did not get there by themselves. There was, as to the gifts, a "Prime Cause." It just turns out that, instead of being the "Supreme Being" (magical Santa) it is merely a "superior" being — Mom and Dad — who, at least at the time of the gifts being given, had greater physical strength, knowledge and autonomy than the dependent child. (And as a further note, one could argue whether or not "Santa Claus" is real even "just a myth," depending on how you define the magical feeling that inspires strangers to give anonymously to those in need at a certain time of the year, but that is further off topic than I want to drift....)

Thus we see that the comparison to Santa Claus actually supports the idea of at least a "superior" being, and relies on the "First Cause."

We see the evidence of *something!* And thus that *something* needs to be accounted for.

And the existence of the created is not the only example of the *something* that needs to be explained. And by way of explanation, there do exist many claims of divine experiences, out of body experiences, near-death experiences and even after-death experiences. While they are not experimental or observable or quantifiable or replicable and thus cannot be consider *scientific* evidence (conforming to a specific form of methodology), that does not mean they are wholly invalid. Subject to individual examination of each specific claim, the credibility of such *anecdotal* evidence needs to be considered on its own merits. *Anecdotal* evidence is not the same as *scientific* evidence, but that does not mean it is necessarily false. Again, subject to challenges to the specific credibility and level of evidentiary support, *anecdotal* evidence is often used as acceptable proof, as in the case of eyewitness testimony in court or as observations of individual instances of observable occurrences that may contribute toward a record of inductively-established patters out of which future deductive probabilities can be inferred.

Betrayal of Jesus

What was the Prime Cause of the "Prime Cause"?

Everything that occurs after the "Big Bang" can be explained by current physics. But the real question, beyond science, as to the question of the "Big Bang," goes back to, what was *before* the "Big Bang"? What caused it to explode? For that matter, what was it? And, whatever it was, what caused it to even exist?

Those who argue for the need of a "Prime Cause," including religious Creationists (or "Intelligent Design" people) using Aristotle's argument, say they have to account for that First Cause, so they define it as "God."

Those questioning the "First Cause" say that, no matter how far back you go, you can't escape the intellectual dilemma of how the "First Cause" got there so, since something had to be there first, save one step (one level of complexity) and eliminate the "First Cause," especially if there is no externally verifiable evidence.

But when we look at the nature of "existence" in the Cosmos, physics tells us that this "existence" is manifest as both "matter" and "energy" and, under the right conditions, they are interchangeable; that is, matter can be converted to energy and, reciprocally, if the conditions are just right, energy can be manifest as matter. In fact, there is no such thing as matter — it is all energy. If you magnify everything to seeing things on a scale at the level of the atom, you see that even the most solid "matter" is comprised of atoms that are actually spaced very far apart, similar to the way in which star systems with their orbiting planets are spaced very far apart from other systems of stars and planets and, within the atom itself, there is massive space separating electrons from each other and from their nucleus, much like the extensive space that separates the planets of our solar system from each other and from the "nucleus" of our solar system, the sun. Yet despite being mostly empty space, the atoms create an illusion of solid matter. And even the spots of density within the atom, the electrons (planets) and nucleus (sun), are not solid the way our planets are solid. They are packets of energy, negatively charged electrons (which generate electricity) revolving around positively charged protons in the nucleus. There is no matter. It is all energy.

So if you look at "existence" prior to the "Big Bang," and try to determine what existed first, which would thus necessarily have to have been both the first "existence" (not "created" by anything else) and therefore the "First Cause" that created everything else that came after itself, what seems most feasible (from pure speculative hypothesis, of course, since this is not observable in any scientific sense) as the nature such form would most likely take: "matter" (the seemingly static or inert form of existence) or "energy" (the active form of existence)?

Something had to be first. Is it more likely that this first existence took the form of static, inert *matter* or active, vibrant, changeable *energy?* It becomes more plausible that the ultimate reality consists of active energy, especially if one considers that, at its most basic levels of existence, matter is, itself, an illusion created by charges of positively- or negatively-charged energy, creating a barrier of resistance that acts like a force field to generate the perception of the "firm rigidity" of matter. There is no distinct entity that exists as "matter" — what we perceive as "matter" is merely an alternative expression of energy. And if one considers the possibility that some energy might be self-existent (since *something* had to be here first), is it that much of a leap to say that what was self-existent could also be self-cognizant or incorporate the origins of consciousness or self direction, even if originating or existing in one of the other dimensions outside our current mortal framework of existence? Further, if one considers the distinction made by religious persons between the physical (material) world and the spiritual dimension, but just exchanges the word "physical" with matter and "spiritual" with energy, the perspective no longer seems so inconsistent with science.

Again, all of this is speculation, *not science,* because it is not observable or quantifiable or replicable, and thus beyond the capacity of the scientific method's protocols of observation, quantification and replacation to address. Thus, I make no claim of authoritative knowledge, but it does seem plausible to consider (especially if one does perceive credible anecdotal "evidence" of interactions with a "higher power") that whatever existed first, and generated everything else, was a form of *energy,* out of which a perception of *matter* could subsequently emerge.

If there is any viable way to incorporate a "First Cause," perhaps it might originate from the interchangeability of matter and energy. But ultimately, this is not knowable in the sense of being provable (or disprovable) by human capabilities of empirical, replicable standards of observation.

Factors to consider

Explaining the universe:

In evaluating the credibility of whether it is feasible, or at least more probably than improbable, to believe in a deity, one must consider that nature of the "higher power" being contemplated. What would such a supreme (or superior) being be like?

Would it have to be the same as what is taught by Christian theologians (or Moslem or Hindu or anything else)?

Is There A God

Would it have to be omnipotent (all-powerful), i.e., a "Supreme" being, or could it just be more powerful than humans subject to its own set of higher limitations, i.e., a "superior" being?

Would it have to be exclusive (i.e., monotheistic)? Could there be many advanced or "superior" beings or energy sources, of varying degrees of power or advancement.

Would it have to be sentient? It might be that the power of the universe consists simply of the forces of physical Laws of Nature — powerful interactions of matter and energy in orderly ways that are more powerful than puny human, and operating in an orderly, predictable adherence to predictable patterns that makes them seem intelligent (or sentient). But just as the powerful winds of tornadoes or hurricanes, or the small steady winds and currents of erosion, or large and small oceanic forces of tsunamis or daily tides shape our world and overpower our comparatively insignificant species, it might also be that there are "higher powers" in the universe, but not in a conscious, sentient or intelligent sense. Or then again, it/they could be extremely intelligent, so far beyond our ability to grasp that we simply fail to perceive it/them, in the same way that ants crawl across our floors without the slightest regard that we "superior" beings are standing over them. Is it even feasible to believe we are the highest power in the universe? The most intelligent? In all those galaxies? In all possible dimensions? It may be feasible to conclude that we are not, even if we merely acknowledge that is a non-verified (non-verifiable) opinion that just feels like the best possible explanation for the things we see beyond what can be known with absolute certainty.

Could the power of the universe, even if unitary in its history and origins, have limitations? That it originates as pure intelligence but limited in its capacity to interact with stimuli, and therefore feels compelled to create a physical universe environment which it then populates with additional sentient, conscious beings which it ignites from its own consciousness as Source but which become distinct and autonomous individual "flames" of separate and independent consciousness, that the original Source can then interact with to expand its capacity for experience? Would the recognition of a higher energy require that it begin its existence already all-powerful and all-complete? If so, why would it have further need or desire to create? If it is already all in all, what purpose would further creation serve? If such a deity exists, there is no reason to require a supposition of omnipotence, omniscience, or omnipresence — only that it be the Original Source and that it be superior, in somewhat the same way that we might perceive our consciousness and intelligence as functioning on a higher plane than that of fruit flies or goldfish while not claiming ourselves to have absolute totally of power, knowledge or presence.

It would certainly be possible to say that one feels there is a better chance for one scenario over another, although lacking definitive evidence or certainty, as long as one recognizes that such opinions are speculative and preferential as distinguished from factual or, in any sense, "proven."

It is further possible to conclude that the need for a First Cause or to explain phenomena that are beyond the scope of human conscious understanding argues for the existence of a "higher power" who is at least superior to humans if not fully supreme (i.e., omnipotent or all-powerful), is more feasible than not coming to that conclusion, without claiming that one knows the details of what that "higher power" is actually like, just as it is also possible to acknowledge that one simply does not know whether or not there is a god.

Explaining spiritual phenomena:

In addition to trying to consider what is the most feasible explanation for the existence of the universe, one must also address the reality of spiritual phenomena.

One must consider that there are many reports of unexplained phenomena that supersede the capacity of human probability or capability. Certainly, many can be debunked as frauds or explained away by identifying more plausible, down-to-earth causes. But not all can be dismissed either as frauds or by alternative explanations. Of course, the fact that we do not have an alternative explanation does not mean that one does not exist, but it also leaves open the door to an explanation that involves a power greater than what is known to or understood by human experience. Often such experiences are "merely" anecdotal one-time occurrences and therefore not quantifiable, measurable or replicable in any way that could be called scientific, and so we must say they are not science, though that does not necessarily make them not valid or in conflict with science, merely outside the boundaries of what science is able to address.

But it is not just the explaining of phenomenological mysteries that needs to be addressed. Such events are rare, and even those who claim to have experienced them with any degree of credibility rarely have more than one or two such occurrences in an entire lifetime.

Beyond such rare experiences are far more common ones: the reality of powerful spiritual or mystical experiences that many people — almost anyone who seeks out such experiences — have attained, and not just once or twice in a lifetime, but on a regular and even frequent basis.

One must account for the powerful spiritual drive that motivates and compels adherence to great faith, whether it be

Betrayal of Jesus

Christians accepting martyrdom or Islamic suicide bombers seeking rewards in a paradisiacal afterlife or the quiet transport to a higher spiritual dimension attained through the meditative arts of Hindu or Buddhist disciplines.

It may be that such experiences arise out of the interplay between conscious and subconscious dimensions of the mind and feelings, or could there be an external associative process involved? Any attempt to address the great questions of cosmology must deal with this facet as well.

On the other hand, those who claim the existence of a deity must account for his/her/its allowance of cruelty and suffering of the innocent, as noted in more detail in Chapter 9. As noted in that section, this might be accommodated by allowing a "higher" or "superior" being rather than one who is fully "omnipotent" or absolutely "supreme" being — just more advanced than us, and "doing the best he/she/it can."

The role of the unknown

When one considers the depth and extent of spiritual phenomena that many have experienced, as well as the anecdotal (distinguished from objectively observable) evidence for something greater than ourselves, it is also important to consider how much of the universe remains unknown to us, and the reasons why certain phenomena can exist that are not only beyond human understanding, but also beyond the capacity for human beings to understand.

There are simply some aspects of the universe that we do not have the ability to process experientially through the senses or into our cognitive functions, and therefore they are unknowable. That does not mean they are not real. To a fly crawling across my computer screen, the information and operations of this technology is simply beyond its capacity to fathom, but that does not make that reality any less real. Some specifics:

Anti-matter: Scientists now have the basis for detecting consequential cosmic "footprints" that suggest evidence of an aspect of the physical universe that we mortal humans are incapable of perceiving directly, known as "anti-matter" or "dark matter." We only know of its existence because it can be deduced from the footprint it leaves in other phenomena that we are able to objectively perceive. Some may find it plausible to consider the possibility that the aspect of spiritual essence could have something to do with this aspect of existence, or that at least in the same way that the existence of anti-matter demonstrates how alternative aspects of the universe can exist, so also spiritual essence could be another such aspect that is only hinted at by spiritual experiences or other unexplained phenomena. Again, lacking objectively quantifiable data, such speculations are conjectural and not scientific, but that does not mean they are not plausible.

Cosmic influence: The key to evolution of life is mutation — small, incremental errors in the reproductive copying of the deoxyribonucleic acid (DNA) molecule. Not surprisingly, most such errors are harmful, because they don't follow the carefully-evolved blueprint. But occasionally, a change is beneficial, conferring survival advantage. What causes such copying errors? One known cause is radiation, the greatest natural source of which are the cosmic rays from outer space that silently but perpetually bombard our existence. Again, purely as speculation, one could imagine that if there is conscious energy guiding the affairs of the universe, and if that consciousness desired to guide the course of development, that every so often it could mandate the occurrence of a specific, desired genetic mutation by influencing a cosmic burst of radiation in just the right genetic location.

Dimensions: Mortal humans operate within three known dimensions of space (height, breadth, depth) and one of time. Physicists report, however, inferential evidence by which the existence of additional dimensions can be deduced, but which are beyond mortal human perception.

One could use the "Flatland" analogy created by Edwin Abbot, a Shakespearean actor who lived in Victorian England. Flatland is an imaginary two-dimensional place whose inhabitants are only able to experience and perceive two physical dimensions, breadth (left-right) and depth (front-back), but no height (up-down). The third dimension exists, but they just can't perceive it. You could have a being (who does experience three physical dimensions) hovering just above them, observing them, and they would be unable to perceive its existence. So, to us in a three-dimensional existence, in which direction from left-right or front-back or up-down would a fourth (or more) dimension exist? We can't say. Additional dimensions (directions) are beyond our capacity to experience. But that does not mean they don't exist; on the contrary, physicists find inferential evidence to conclude that they do. As to where they are or what they are, coming to any conclusions is purely speculative. But, again, it is also possible to speculate that the link to spiritual aspects of the universe that we cannot experience in our current physical limitations, may be experienced in spiritual dimensions. It is possible to speculate that, beyond death, we return to our connection to additional dimensions and may be able to see and experience aspects of the universe that may be very close to us, but are not perceivable in our current state. And again, such conclusions are purely speculative, as we do not have the means by which to empirically test them. That does not mean they are not plausible.

Mind —> body dichotomy: There has long been debate as to whether the mind (soul) is a separate entity from the body (brain), or whether it is an illusion created out of the synaptic connections of the brain. Does the mind (the conscious process of mental and emotional experience) exist separately from the physical properties of the brain (a bodily organ)? Or is the illusion of a mind created out of purely physical, biological properties? Is it possible that an entity of experiential energy can exist as a link between the domains of matter and energy, or possibly a link from some other dimension to this one, in ways not observable, quantifiable or measurable by purely physical or objectively scientific means? Or is the illusion of such a figment created by the physical? One thing can be said with certainty: the perception of distinctly separate entities of physical and experiential clearly does exist. Whether we conclude that the more plausible probability favors the duality or the singularity (neither of which can be proven with certainty), from a perspective of how we deal with the relationship between the mind (soul) and the body (brain), we must do so recognizing the way it is perceived experientially.

Conclusions

It is impossible, in this mortal existence, to know with absolute certainty or in empirical and measurable (i.e., scientific) terms, how the universe came to exist and whether or not that coming into existence involved the guidance of an intelligent force of energy or if it simply occurred as a matter of random chance.

We can, however, speculate as to which of various possibilities seem more probable or plausible or reasonable, as long as we do not forget that such contemplations are just that: speculation. They are not questions of science, they cannot be answered by scientific protocols and they do not belong in the realm of science. They are matters of spiritual conjecture and philosophical speculation.

We must further consider that, if there is a deity at the center of creation and existence, this god has chosen to hide from us. None of the many claims of divine revelation, personal interactions with gods, or supposed claims of proof for his/her/its existence withstands thorough scrutiny. There may be credible or plausible reasons why such a deity would choose to, at least in this time and place of mortal experience, remain elusive, but our contemplation of any rational view about the existence of god must recognize that he/she/it has chosen to remain unknowable to any degree of certainty, at least for this phase of our existence. We can further acknowledge that being elusive does not mean being nonexistent. Scattered here and there among the widespread hype, hoopla and hoax arise occasional glimmers of credible, plausible anecdotal (not scientific or replicable) experience with the divine, or at least that which transcends known mortal experience. It may be that, whatever deity(ies) or higher power(s) there may be, do not allow a general revelation of knowledge for public consumption, but will permit personal, individual experience in a personal, individual way to those who encounter the right path toward seeking it.

But no matter what is "out there," those who do seek it do find something very real. We must recognize the importance of taking that reality seriously, whether it be the reality of something fashioned in the depths of our subconsciousnesses, or something literally external to ourselves.

Whatever it is, there is something that people do find when they seek the spiritual dimension of our existence. Whatever it is, it is an important part of the human experience.

About the Author

Davis D. Danizier is a humble seeker of truth, now approaching sixty years of age, raised and still living in Southern California.

Dave Danizier was raised in a household that was religiously and politically conservative and embraced these traditions and was active in teen Bible study activities through adolescence and early college years. Eventually, based on his own encounters with scriptural study and with exposure to insights and writings of others, he became aware of contradictions and rational flaws and scientific errors represented in Christian teaching and scriptures and eventually recognized that, like many other great religions of the world, despite its many positive aspects, it could not be accepted as the divine and singular path to "salvation."

Politically, Dave Danizier is not registered with any particular political party, but tends to support candidates and issues that are progressive. His primary interest, and the focus of his commentaries, is in debunking religious mythologies while also respectfully expressing appreciation for the important historical, ethical and cultural contributions of the great literature that originated out of religious traditions and which has shaped our civilization in both positive and negative ways.

Betrayal of Jesus

www.ingramcontent.com/pod-product-compliance
Lightning Source LLC
Chambersburg PA
CBHW051434290426
44109CB00016B/1554